Using Corpora in the Language Learning Classroom
CORPUS LINGUISTICS FOR TEACHERS

Gena R. Bennett

Ann Arbor
University of Michigan Press

ISBN-13: 978-0-472-03385-0

2013   2012   2011   2010   4   3   2   1

Preface

──────────────────────── The idea behind this teacher resource book is founded in the words of some of corpus linguistics' most prominent researchers. In his plenary address "Corpus Linguistics and Language Teaching: The Next Lexus" at the 2005 TESOL convention, Biber stated that two problems plague the progression of corpus linguistics in language teaching: (1) adapting corpus findings to classroom materials and (2) determining the most effective applications to classroom teaching. Also, Sinclair says that "to make good use of corpus resources a teacher needs a modest orientation to the routines involved in retrieving information from the corpus, and—most importantly—training and experience in how to evaluate that information" (Sinclair, 2004, p. 2). In addition, Conrad says, "the strongest force for change [regarding corpus linguistics and language teaching] could be a generation of ESL teachers who were introduced [to corpus linguistics] in their training programs, who appreciate the scope of the work, and who have practiced developing their own corpus research and activities in classrooms" (Conrad, 2000, p. 556).

Using Corpora in the Language Learning Classroom is intended for practicing teachers who want to use corpora in the classroom. It can also be used by graduate students who are studying applied linguistics or TESOL. The goal of this book is to make the ideas of corpus linguistics accessible to teachers and, most important, provide ideas, instruction, and opportunities for teachers to use the applications of corpus linguistics in their classrooms.

Using Corpora in the Language Learning Classroom is divided into three parts. Each part begins with an introduction, which provides background knowledge applicable to the ideas discussed in that part. Part 1, An Introduction to Corpus Linguistics, contains a brief look at the theory and principles of corpus linguistics. This part provides readers with a brief, but thorough, background to understand the methodology behind the activities shared in the book. Part 2, Corpora in Language Teaching, introduces three tiers of applied corpus linguistics and begins the discussion of applications to the classroom. Part 3, Corpus-Designed Activities, focuses specifically on corpus-designed activities, including those activities you can use directly in the classroom. It is worth noting that each chapter in Part 3 is titled based on specific comments students made after completing some of these activities in their classes.

Using Corpora in the Language Learning Classroom includes eight chapters. The Target Feature(s) sections detail the language features that are addressed in the activities. Many of these details are taken from the *Longman Grammar of Spoken and Written English* (Biber et al., 1999). The Tools sections explain what materials are necessary for the activity and present a brief overview for general use of each. The Procedures sections provide step-by-step instructions for carrying out the activities in addition to pointers for creating similar activities. The On Your Own sections suggest activities for exploring corpora and corpus tools on your own.

The appendices contain an index of corpora/corpus tools that can be utilized in the language classroom and reproducible materials to accompany the activities presented in Chapters 4–7.

It is not a goal of this book to provide a complete theoretical foundation for corpus linguistics. For such a foundation, I suggest reading *From Corpus to Classroom* (O'Keeffe, McCarthy, & Carter, 2007) or *Corpora in Applied Linguistics* (Hunston, 2002). *Using Corpora* does, however, provide its readers with the basic theoretical underpinnings needed to work with corpora in the classroom. After engaging in this text, my hope is that readers feel encouraged in their understanding of the principles of corpus linguistics and equipped in their knowledge of the applications of corpus linguistics for the classroom to more effectively and efficiently enable students to acquire a second language.

Acknowledgments

I am forever grateful to my colleagues who have worked with me developing ideas for applications of corpus linguistics in the classroom, specifically Meredith Bricker, as well as instructors who encouraged and challenged me at various presentations I conducted on using corpus linguistics in the classroom. This book has been a pleasure to write, and I hope is as much a pleasure to read, and, more importantly, as much a pleasure to implement its ideas in your classrooms.

Grateful acknowledgment is made to the following authors, publishers, and individuals for permission to reprint previously published materials beyond fair use guidelines.

Cambridge University Press for material on pages 25 and 98 in *Touchstone 1 Student Book* by M. McCarthy, J. McCarten, and H. Sandiford, copyright © 2005.

Averil Coxhead for permission to use the Academic Word list and the website: www.victoria.ac.nz/lals/staff/averil-coxhead/awl/mostfreq1.html.

Mark Davies for screen shots from the Corpus of Contemporary American English (COCA). Used with permission. http://corpus.byu.edu.

Dr. Matthias Hüning of the Institut für Deutsche und Niederländische Philologie for screen shots from TextSTAT. Used with permission. http://neon.niederlandistik.fu-berlin.de/en/textstat/.

Contents

Acronyms

ANC—American National Corpus
AOR—Amazon Online Reader
AWL—Academic Word List
BLC—Business Letter Corpus
BNC—British National Corpus
CANDLE—Corpora and Natural Language Processing for the Digital Learning
   of English
CDA—Corpus-designed Activity
CEA—Computer-Aided Error Analysis
CGE—Cambridge Grammar of English
CHILDES—Child Language Data Exchange System
CIC—Cambridge International Corpus
COCA—Corpus of Contemporary American English
CUP—Cambridge University Press
DDL—Data Driven Learning
EAP—English for Academic Purposes
ESP—English for Specific Purposes
ETC—Error Tagging Code
ICLE—International Corpus of Learner English
IRB—Internal Review Board
LGWSE—Longman Grammar of Written and Spoken English
LSWEC—Longman Spoken and Written English Corpus
MICASE—Michigan Corpus of Academic Spoken English
MICUSP—Michigan Corpus of Upper-level Student Papers
OCD—Oxford Collocations Dictionary
SST—Standard Speaking Test
TextSTAT—Simple Text Analysis Tool
UMP—University of Michigan Press

PART 1

AN INTRODUCTION
TO CORPUS LINGUISTICS

——————————————— The principles of corpus linguistics have been around for almost a century. Lexicographers, or dictionary makers, have been collecting examples of language in use to help accurately define words since at least the late 19th century. Before computers, these examples of language were essentially collected on small slips of paper and organized in pigeon holes. The advent of computers led to the creation of what we consider to be modern-day corpora. The first computer-based corpus, the Brown corpus, was created in 1961 and comprised about 1 million words. Today, generalized corpora are hundreds of millions of words in size, and corpus linguistics is making outstanding contributions to the fields of second language research and teaching.

WHAT IS CORPUS LINGUISTICS?

So what exactly is corpus linguistics? Corpus linguistics approaches the study of language in use through corpora (singular: *corpus*). A corpus is a large, principled collection of naturally occurring examples of language stored electronically. In short, corpus linguistics serves to answer two fundamental research questions:

1. What particular patterns are associated with lexical or grammatical features?
2. How do these patterns differ within varieties and registers?

Many notable scholars, have, of course, contributed to the development of modern-day corpus linguistics: Leech, Biber, Johansson, Francis, Hunston, Conrad, and McCarthy, to name just a few. These scholars have made substantial contributions to corpus linguistics, both past and present. Many corpus linguists, however, consider John Sinclair to be one of, if not the most, influential scholar of modern-day corpus linguistics. Sinclair detected that a word in and of itself does not carry meaning, but that meaning is often made through several words in a sequence (Sinclair, 1991). This is the idea that forms the backbone of corpus linguistics.

WHAT CORPUS LINGUISTICS IS NOT

It's important to not only understand what corpus linguistics is, but also what corpus linguistics is <u>not</u>. Corpus linguistics is not

- able to provide negative evidence
- able to explain why
- able to provide all possible language at one time.

Corpus linguistics is not able to provide negative evidence. This means a corpus can't tell us what's possible or correct or not possible or incorrect in language; it can only tell us what is or is not present in the corpus. Many instructors mistakenly believe that if a corpus does not present all manners to express a certain idea, then the corpus is altogether faulty. Instead, instructors should believe that if a corpus does not present a particular manner to express a certain idea, then perhaps that manner is not very common in the register represented by the corpus.

Corpus linguistics is not able to explain why something is the way it is, only tell us what is. To find out why, we, as users of language, use our intuition.

Corpus linguistics is not able to provide all possible language at one time. By definition, a corpus should be principled: "a large, *principled* collection of naturally occurring texts. . .," meaning that the language that goes into a corpus isn't random, but planned. However, no matter how planned, principled, or large a corpus is, it cannot be a representative of all language. In other words, even in a corpus that contains one billon words, such as the Cambridge International Corpus (CIC), all instances of use of a language may not be present.

Chapter 1

Principles of Corpus Linguistics

QUESTIONS WE CAN ANSWER WITH CORPORA

Broadly, corpus linguistics looks to see what patterns are associated with lexical and grammatical features. Searching corpora provides answers to questions like these:

- What are the most frequent words and phrases in English?
- What are the differences between spoken and written English?
- What tenses do people use most frequently?
- What prepositions follow particular verbs?
- How do people use words like *can, may*, and *might*?
- Which words are used in more formal situations and which are used in more informal ones?
- How often do people use idiomatic expressions?
- How many words must a learner know to participate in everyday conversation?
- How many different words do native speakers generally use in conversation? (McCarthy, 2004, pp. 1–2)

For the most part, these questions don't look particularly revolutionary. We already know the answers to a lot of them. We teach the ideas contained within many of these questions every day. We can open up almost any grammar, vocabulary, conversation, or writing textbook and find the answers. Even better, we can apply our expert-user intuition to find the answers. We're intimately connected to the language; after all, we speak it every day, right? An exercise may help here. For example, O'Keeffe, McCarthy, and Carter (2007, p. 32) studied a frequency list from a 10 million–word corpus and discovered that the 2,000 most frequent words in the corpus accounted for 80 percent of all the

> A **frequency list** displays the words occurring in a corpus along with the number of times each word appears.

words present. A mere 2 percent of the words were used repeatedly to account for 8 million words.

For example, degree adverbs demonstrate the extent of a particular feature, such as *thoroughly* in the sentence, *Her chocolate cake is thoroughly delicious*. Keep this in mind, and think for a moment about these questions.

▶ What are some common adverbs of degree? Think of at least four.

▶ Give examples of ways you would use these adverbs.

▶ Which adverbs do you think are used more often in speaking?

▶ Which adverbs do you think are used more often in writing?

▶ Which adverbs do you think are used more often overall?

You may have thought of these, among others:

■ ***very***—*My sister is very intelligent.*

■ ***really***—*Listening to an in-class lecture can be really difficult.*

■ ***exactly***—*Sue always knows exactly what I'm thinking.*

■ ***quite***—*Frederick appeared quite surprised by the low mark on his project.*

■ ***completely***—*The surprise birthday party was completely unexpected.*

■ ***too***—*Working full time and going to school full time is too demanding for my schedule.*

From this list of adverbs, we might think that *really* is used more in speaking and *quite* is used more in writing. Perhaps *very* is used most frequently overall.

The exercise used multiple adverbs of degree: where they're used, the frequency of use, and some examples of use. This information seems like sufficient material for a lesson, and most teachers would feel comfortable presenting this information in class.

Corpora can give us information like frequency, register, and how language is used, ideas identified in the adverbs of degree exercise.

Table 1.1 shows the frequency results per million (rounded to the nearest one) from the Corpus of Contemporary American English (COCA). (See Appendix 1 for

Because corpora don't contain the same number of words, we can't use a simple frequency count to see in which corpus a word is more common. For example, *very* occurs in the spoken portion of the Corpus of Contemporary American English (COCA) 195,000 times and in the written portion of the COCA 198,000 times; from looking only at the simple frequency count, we might conclude that *very* is used only slightly more in written language. But, because the written portion of the COCA is much larger than the spoken portion, we can only get an accurate comparison by calculating how many times *very* occurs per million words. This is the **normed count**. The normed counts in Table 1.1 show that for every million words in the spoken portion of the COCA, *very* appears 2,543 times; for every million words in the written portion, *very* only appears 673 times. This allows us to see that, in fact, *very* is used significantly more frequently in the spoken portion of the corpus than in the written portion of the corpus.

more information on this and other corpora. COCA will also be discussed in Chapter 4.) The numbers in the Speak column indicate how many times the adverbs *very, really, exactly, quite, completely, too,* and *thoroughly* are used in the spoken portion of the COCA. The numbers in the Write column indicate how many times the adverbs are used in the written portion of the COCA, and the numbers in the TOTAL columns indicate how many times the adverbs are used overall.

Very is the most frequently used adverb overall in the COCA, and is especially frequent in spoken language. *Really* is the second most frequent adverb in speaking and overall, while *too* is the most frequent adverb used in writing. Note that *too* and *completely* are used almost the same in speaking and as in writing. With the exception of *thoroughly*, and to a significantly lesser degree *too*, these adverbs of degree are used more frequently in spoken language than written language.

Visit www.americancorpus.org/ to complete your own search on **adverbs of degree.**

So what does all this mean? These data present us with opportunities to show students more accurately how to use language. When teaching adverbs of degree, based on the information from this corpus, it would be prudent to emphasize the following:

▶ Focus attention on *really* and *very* because they are the most commonly used adverbs of degree, and students will likely encounter them often.

▶ Point out that *too* and *completely* are different from *really* and *very* because they are used almost equally in speaking and writing.

▶ Show how *thoroughly* is used differently because it appears more frequently in writing than in speaking (the only adverb here to significantly do so).

Table 1.1
Frequency Results Per Million of Adverbs of Degree in COCA

Word	Speak	Write	Total
very	2,543	673	3,216
really	1,637	392	2,029
exactly	271	93	364
quite	267	150	417
completely	87	78	165
too	656	699	1,355
thoroughly	7	18	25
Total	5,468	2,103	7571

Source: Corpus of Contemporary American English

▶ Use more listening and speaking activities to teach adverbs of degree because these particular adverbs are used more than two times more in speaking than writing.

In a nutshell, corpus linguistics allows us to see how language is used today and how that language is used in different contexts, enabling us to teach language more effectively.

THE CORPUS APPROACH

Is corpus linguistics a methodology? Is it theory? Most corpus linguists are not willing to answer that question in such terms, but when analyzing language using corpora, there is a "method" to employ.

The Corpus Approach (Biber, Conrad, & Reppen, 1998, p. 4) is comprised of four major characteristics:

1️⃣ It is empirical, analyzing the actual patterns of language use in natural texts.

2️⃣ It utilizes a large and principled collection of natural texts as the basis for analysis.

3️⃣ It makes extensive use of computers for analysis.

4️⃣ It depends on both quantitative and qualitative analytical techniques.

1. The Corpus Approach is empirical, analyzing the actual patterns of language use in natural texts.

The key to this characteristic of the Corpus Approach is authentic language. The idea that corpora are principled has been mentioned but not what language a corpus is comprised of. Corpora are composed from textbooks, fiction, nonfiction, magazines, academic papers, world literature, newspapers, telephone conversations at home or work, cell phone conversations, business meetings, class lectures, radio broadcasts, and TV shows, among other communication acts. In short, any real-life situation in which any linguistic communication takes place can form a corpus.

2. The Corpus Approach utilizes a large and principled collection of naturally occurring texts as the basis for analysis.

This characteristic of the Corpus Approach refers to the corpus itself. You may work with a written corpus, a spoken corpus, an academic spoken corpus, etc.

3. The Corpus Approach makes extensive use of computers for analysis.

Not only do computers hold corpora, they help analyze the language in a corpus. A corpus is accessed and analyzed by a concordancing program. In short, you can't effectively utilize corpora, or employ the corpus approach, without a computer.

4. The Corpus Approach depends on both quantitative and qualitative analytical techniques.

This characteristic of the corpus approach highlights the importance of our intuition as expert users of a language. We take the quantitative results generated from the corpus and then analyze them qualitatively to find significance. Table 1.1 shows quantitative results. Qualitatively analyzing the results would involve examining the adverbs of degree in use to understand situations the adverbs are used in. This is how we answer the question *Why?*

TARGET FEATURES

Although intuition may not always be reliable for drawing conclusions about language in general, it does often answer the question *Why?* Intuition is often useful for helping us form queries for a corpus. Many of the questions that corpora answers fall into certain areas of language teaching, such as phraseology, lexicogrammar, registers, English for Specific Purposes (ESP), nuances of language, and appropriate syllabus design.

Phraseology

Phraseology is the study of phrases. Phraseology is a central element of corpus linguistics: Sinclair (1991) determined that the meaning of a word is found through several words in a sequence, through phrases. Phraseology includes the study of collocations, lexical bundles, and language occurring in preferred sequences.

Collocation

The most prominent way of studying phrases is through collocation. Collocation is the statistical tendency of words to co-occur. This means that when one word is used, there is a high statistical probability that a certain word or words will occur alongside of it. For example, look at the noun form of the word *deal*. The words *big, good,* and *great* are collocations of *deal* as a noun, meaning that when we use *deal* as a noun, we often refer to a *big deal*, a *good deal*, and/or a *great deal*. From studying collocations, we know that there is a tendency for each collocate of a word to be associated with a single sense of that word. We can see this looking at the phrases using *deal*—*big deal, good deal, great deal*: a *big deal* is usually an event or situation that has significant meaning; a *good deal* generally refers to a bargain; a *great deal* often refers to a quantity. Studying collocations provides a deeper understanding of the meaning and use of a word, such as *deal*, than simply studying a word alone.

Collocations can also help us better understand particular words used in a certain phrase. Kennedy (1991) studied *between* and *through*, something many language textbooks have difficulty distinguishing the use of. By studying the collocations of the two words, Kennedy found that *between* is usually used after nouns like *differences, distinction, agreement*, and *meeting*, whereas *through* is more frequently found after verbs such as *go, pass, run*, and *fall* (1991, p. 107). (Chapter 3 of this book presents an activity dealing with collocation.)

Lexical Bundles

Phraseology also looks at variation in somewhat fixed phrases, which are often referred to as lexical bundles. Biber, Johansson, Leech, Conrad, and Finegan (1999, p. 990) define a lexical bundle as a recurring sequence of three or more words. In conversation, "Do you want me to" and "I don't know what" are among the most common lexical bundles (Biber et al., 1999, p. 994). It is important to understand that lexical bundles are different from idioms. Idioms have a meaning not derivable from their parts, unlike lexical bundles, which do. Also, lexical bundles are not complete phrases. Most important, lexical bundles are statistically defined (identified by their overwhelming co-occurrence), and idioms are not.

One type of lexical bundle is a frame. A frame has set words around a variable word or words. One example of the use of frames is the expression of future time. In the Corpus of Contemporary American English, multiple words are used to express future time using the frame *is…to*: *is going to, is likely to, is expected to, is supposed to, is about to, is due to. Is* and *to* are the set words of the frame that surround the variables like *going likely, expected,* or *about*.

Preferred Sequences

Phraseology also includes the study of preferred sequences of words. Look at the adjectives *interested* and *interesting*. Hunston (2002, pp. 9–11) explains that learners often confuse these two words, and explanations of their different meanings do not usually help students use the words correctly; looking at the phrases *someone is interested in something, an interesting thing, what is interesting*, and *it is interesting to see,* can give students the ability to use the individual words correctly by providing an established pattern of use for each word.

Only through corpus study can we find the details of phraseology—collocations, lexical bundles, and language occurring in preferred sequences.

Lexicogrammar

Another area of language teaching that corpus linguistics addresses is lexicogrammar. Lexicogrammar is Sinclair's (1991) idea that there is no difference between lexis and grammar, or that lexis and grammar are so closely intertwined that they cannot be productively studied separately. Certain lexical items fall in certain patterns and certain patterns contain certain lexical items.

> To see the **most common patterns** for verbs, nouns, or adjectives, visit http:// candle.cs.nthu.edu.tw/collocation/ webform2.aspx?funcID=9.

An example of the idea of lexicogrammar includes certain words (lexicon) associated with certain verbs tenses (grammar): *know, matter*, and *suppose* occur more than 80 percent of the time in the present tense while *smile, reply,* and *pause* occur more than 80 percent in the past tense (Biber et al., 1999, p. 459). We can also find that some verbs are used most frequently in certain clauses: *know* and *think* are associated with *that*-complement clauses (Biber et al., 1999, p. 661), while the verbs *like, want,* and *seem* are associated with *to*-complement clauses (Biber et al., 1999, pp. 699).

Hunston and Francis (2000, p. 1–2) offer us a more detailed example.

> ❶ Philosophy is different from many other disciplines ❷ in that learning about it is as much a matter of developing skills (in reasoning and argument) as it is a matter of learning a body of information. ❸ In this sense there are no definitive 'answers' to many philosophical problems: ❹ becoming a philosopher is a matter of becoming able to reason coherently and relevantly about philosophical issues. ❺ Consequently, valuable contact time with lecturers is best spent actually 'doing philosophy,' ❻ and that means actively thinking and talking about it.

The word *matter* appears three times in the paragraph. What is happening in each usage?

a matter of developing skills

a matter of learning a body of information

a matter of becoming able to reason coherently and relevantly

a matter of + -ing.

In this sense or use of *matter*, it's much more productive to teach the pattern *a matter of + -ing* rather than to focus on the single lexical word *matter*.

Register

The third area of language teaching that corpus linguistics addresses is register. Register is defined as situation of use.[1] We use different language with different audiences—our parents, colleagues, or children—at different times and for different reasons. Register can be broadly defined—spoken versus written—or more narrowly defined—conversation versus news or even separate parts of a research paper.

Corpus linguistics addresses language teaching through the study of registers by illustrating the various phraseology and lexicogrammar used from register to register. For example, 90 percent of lexical bundles in conversation are declarative or interrogative clauses (Biber et al., 1999, p. 999); pronouns are used slightly more in conversation than nouns, but nouns are used significantly more than pronouns in fiction, news, and academic writing (Biber et al., 1999, p. 235); past tense is used more in writing and present tense more in conversation (Biber et al., 1999, p. 456). In different registers, corpora show us differences of use in language such as word frequency, word meaning and use, and grammatical frequency.

ESP (English for Specific Purposes)

ESP is probably one of the most obvious and pointed applications of corpus linguistics. The areas of register, lexicogrammar, and phraseology can all be applied to specific purposes.

The Academic Word List (AWL) (Coxhead, 2000) is a well-known example of using corpus linguistics to address ESP, in this case, academic purposes. By investigating a corpus comprised of academic language, Coxhead was able to pinpoint the most frequent vocabulary words used in academic texts; she then made the list available for instructors to help students focus their vocabulary study. A project is also underway to further that study by investigating the phraseology and lexicogrammatical patterns of the top words on the AWL (Byrd, 2007).

> Visit the official **AWL** website: www.victoria.ac.nz/lals/staff/averil-coxhead/awl/.

Like the corpus created using academic texts to compile the AWL, corpora can be created and investigated for a myriad of purposes. Right now corpora exist for nurses and health care professionals, air traffic controllers, and switchboard operators, just to name a few. Iowa State University has used a corpus of research articles for each major of its graduate students in order to help them write research articles in their designated field (Cortes, 2007).

> The **BLC (Business Letters Corpus)** is an ESP corpus. You can search the BLC to explore language used by Japanese business people writing business letters at www.someya-net.com/concordancer/.

---

1. The terms *register* and *genre* are often interchangeable in corpus studies.

Nuances of Language

Another area that corpus linguistics addresses in language teaching is nuances of language; like ESP, nuances of language are also a sort of combination of the areas of language teaching addressed by corpus linguistics that have already been discussed. This is the contribution to teaching that, in my experiences, many language instructors seem to appreciate the most.

Nuances of language refer to questions that students might ask that we just don't know the answers to. Often, the questions specifically relate to areas of collocation and frequency. Our response, as teachers, is usually something like, "There is no difference/such thing" or "That's just the way it is in English," which isn't particularly helpful. For example, what if a student says, "I stubbed my large toe." That doesn't sound exactly right. Why? Well, that's just not the way we say it in English. When do you use *is not* (or *'s not*) versus *isn't*? We're likely to tell students that there's probably not really any difference between the two. But, corpus linguistics can answer both these questions. McCarthy (2004, p. 4) found that *is not* is used more with pronouns and *isn't* with nouns. And large toe? We use *large* to describe quantity and *big* to describe physical size, so *big toe* it is.

Syllabus Design

The final area of language teaching that corpus linguistics addresses is syllabus design. Phraseology, lexicogrammar, register, ESP, nuances of language—all of these areas can be used to more accurately and effectively design syllabi by helping us see what students really need to know about language: frequency and collocation for vocabulary, grammar patterns for different registers, and specific knowledge for specific purposes. And what are accurate descriptions of it. For example, the present perfect appears in almost every grammar textbook. It's usually defined as "recent past" or "completed action." However, a corpus study revealed that more than 80 percent of the time, present perfect is used to signify "indefinite past" (Mindt, 2000, p. 224). Statistics of this kind help textbook writers, course designers, and teachers set priorities for the classroom. If you, as a teacher, are armed with this kind of knowledge, you can supplement course materials with information that is relevant for students.

TOOLS

Types of Corpora

A corpus is a principled collection of authentic texts stored electronically that can be used to discover information about language that may not have been noticed through intuition alone. When you want to consult a corpus, what exactly should you look for? This is a very important question.

Because most published materials based on corpora make use of large, general corpora, many readers may believe this is the type of corpus that can be useful in the classroom. Actually, there are approximately eight types of corpora—generalized, specialized, learner, pedagogic, historical, parallel, comparable, and monitor—and which type should be used depends on the purpose for the corpus; only the four types of corpora that are most useful for employing the corpus approach directly in the classroom will be discussed here.

Generalized Corpora

The broadest type of corpus is a generalized corpus. Generalized corpora are often very large, more than 10 million words, and contain a variety of language so that findings from it may be somewhat generalized. Although no corpus will ever represent all possible language, generalized corpora seek to give users as much of a whole picture of a language as possible. The British National Corpus (BNC) and the American National Corpus (ANC) are examples of large, generalized corpora. The COCA is also an example of a generalized corpus. These large, generalized corpora contain written texts such as newspaper and magazine articles, works of fiction and nonfiction, as well as writing from scholarly journals; these corpora also contain spoken transcripts such as informal conversations, government proceedings, and business meetings. If generalizations about language as a whole are to be drawn, a large, general corpus should be consulted.

Specialized Corpora

A specialized corpus contains texts of a certain type and aims to be representative of the language of this type. Specialized corpora can be large or small and are often created to answer very specific questions. Examples of specialized corpora include the Michigan Corpus of Academic Spoken English (MICASE), which contains only spoken language from a university setting; the CHILDES Corpus (MacWhinney, 1992), which contains language used by children; the MICUSP, Michigan Corpus of Upper-level Student Papers, a collection of papers from a range of university disciplines; and a medical corpus containing language used by nurses and hospital staff. Specialized corpora are often used in ESP settings. The AWL, for example, was generated from a specialized corpora of academic texts.

Learner Corpora

A learner corpus is a kind of specialized corpus that contains written texts and/or spoken transcripts of language used by students who are currently acquiring the language. Learner corpora are often tagged and can be examined, for example, to see common errors students made. A well-known learner corpus is the International Corpus of Learner English (ICLE) (Granger, 2003), which contains essays written by English language learners with 14 different native languages. While the ICLE is more generalized, containing writings from learners with 14 different native languages, other learner corpora are more specialized; for example, the Standard Speaking Test Corpus (SST), comprised of oral interview tests of Japanese learners. Targeted instruction can be developed for general language teaching or for specific language groups depending on the type of learner corpus. Chapter 7 will look at corpus-designed activities created from a learner corpus.

> When a corpus is **tagged,** each word included in the corpus has a marker added to it that gives additional information. Often, tags are part of speech markers, enabling users of corpora to search not only for specific words, but also for specific words used as a particular part of speech.

Pedagogic Corpora

A pedagogic corpus is a corpus that contains language used in classroom settings. Pedagogic corpora can include academic textbooks, transcripts of classroom interactions, or any other written text or spoken transcript that learners encounter in an educational setting. Pedagogic corpora can be used to ensure students are learning useful language, to examine teacher-student dynamics, or as a self-reflective tool for teacher development.

Creating Corpora

A corpus is a principled collection of authentic texts stored electronically. When creating a corpus, there must be a focus on three factors: the corpus must be principled, it must use authentic texts, and it must have the ability to be stored electronically.

A corpus is principled, meaning that the language comprising the corpus cannot be random but chosen according to specific characteristics. Having a principled corpus is especially important for more narrow investigations; for example, if you want your students to look at the use of signal words in academic speech, then it's important that the corpus used is comprised of only academic speech. A principled corpus is also necessary for larger, more general corpora, especially in instances where users may want to make generalizations based on their findings. In creating the Longman Spoken and Written English Corpus (LSWEC), a 40 million–word corpus created to identify and understand grammatical patterns in English—the corpus that the information in the *Longman Grammar of Spoken and Written English* (Biber et al., 1999) is based on—

the compilers included a representative sampling from conversation, fiction, news, and academic prose. Whatever the purpose of the corpus, it must be principled.

A corpus must also include authentic texts. Although there is debate over the definition of "authentic" texts in second language teaching (see Widdowson, 1990, for example), for purposes of this discussion, authentic texts are defined as those that are used for a genuine communicative purpose. In the MICASE, only speech acts that naturally occurred in the course of routine daily events at a university are included. The LSWEC includes texts from daily newspapers that were distributed and conversations that took place during participants' weekly routines. The main idea behind the authenticity of the corpus is that the language it contains is not made up for the sole purpose of creating the corpus.

Lastly, a corpus is stored electronically. Corpora can be saved in text format (.txt), rich text format (.rtf), and/or web-based format (.html), or others, depending on the concordancing program used to access texts. The electronic storage and easy accessibility of texts is one of the major factors that allows corpus linguistics to be applied in the classroom.

If you are creating your own corpus, one way to gather principled, authentic texts that can be stored electronically is through Internet "alerts." Search engines such as Yahoo and Google gather email updates of the latest relevant results based on a topic or specific query generated by the user. Alerts can be used to monitor a developing news story, keep current on a particular theme, get the latest on a celebrity or event, and/or keep tabs on a favorite sports team; an example is shown in Figure 1.1. One way to use corpora created from alerts is to investigate common vocabulary used in certain topics, such as frequent content words used in articles that discuss the environment.

Another means of gathering principled, authentic texts that can be stored electronically is looking at Internet essay sites. Many of the academic essay sites have a disclaimer that their essays should be used for research purposes only, and should not to be downloaded or turned in as one's own work. These sites can be very helpful for creating corpora specific for academic writing with term papers, essays, and reports on subjects such as business, literature, art, history, and science. You can even access essay sites that aren't academic. The creation of a corpus using essays from NPR's "This I Believe" program can be analyzed for American viewpoints and language, for example.

Corpora can also be created from resources at hand. Textbooks can be used to create a pedagogic corpus to investigate the language of academic textbooks. This would be especially useful for students enrolled in an Intensive English Program (IEP) or an English for Academic Purposes (EAP) program. Learner corpora can be created from the compilation of student work taken from one particular class, for one particular student, or from a series of students and classes. Students can analyze their own language use and pinpoint areas that need further instruction or document progress that has been made.

Figure 1.1
Google Alerts

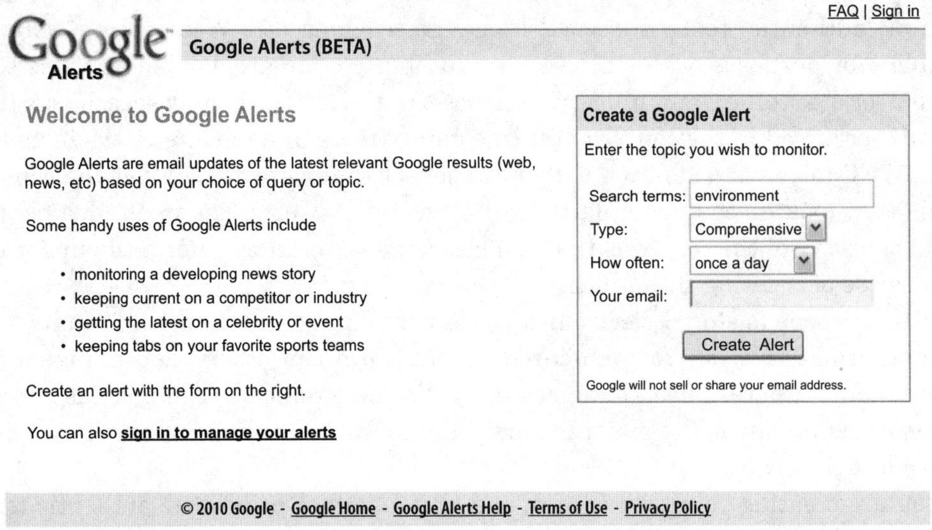

Google Alerts allow users to collect email updates based on a specific topic or query as shown here. You can choose register, news, blogs, the web, videos, groups, or all of the above (as shown). Either once a day (as shown), as it happens, or once a week, text will be emailed that relates to a specified topic. These texts can be combined to investigate vocabulary or grammar patterns, for example, for particular themes.

An important aspect related to creating corpora is the issue of copyright, especially if findings from a corpus will be distributed via a handout or published in any form. Contact Internet sites for their permissions policy, and always get students' written permission before using their work for any purpose. Some institutions may also require you to complete an Internal Review Board (IRB) application for a corpus study.

An institution's IRB serves to monitor research involving human subjects. The role of the IRB is paramount in medical studies during which physical or psychological damage may be done to research participants, although studies involving research of normal educational practices—such as those concerning instructional strategies or the effectiveness or comparisons of instructional methods—can often be exempted so long as a clear demonstration can be made that human subjects will not be identified (e.g., the use of numbers instead of names or the keeping of research documents in locked drawers). **Copyright is a serious issue and should not be overlooked.**

Concordancing Programs

Two tools are needed to effectively apply corpus linguistics in the classroom: the corpus and the concordancing program. Concordancing programs are computer software used to access and sort data from the corpus. Most large corpora, like the MICASE, have a built-in concordancing program. When the concordancing program is built in, as is the instance with the MICASE, only the search options are important to understand for the program. See Figure 1.2 for search options in the MICASE concordancer.

When you create your own corpora or want to access a corpus that does not have a built-in concordancing program, it's important to note that many effective concordancing programs are available. Some concordancing programs are very affordable, and others are free.

A concordancing program should be chosen based on what information you want from your corpus. On the basic level, all concordancing programs provide a frequency list that provides each word used in the corpus as well as the number of times the word appears in the corpus. Often, the list can be sorted by frequency or alphabetically. In addition, most concordancing programs show concordance lines from the corpus. Concordance lines are all the instances of a word or phrase in the corpus. Many concordancing programs will allow you to sort the concordance lines according to what comes before or after a specified word or phrase and will let you see more extended context of the word as it appears in the corpus.

Figure 1.2
The MICASE Corpus

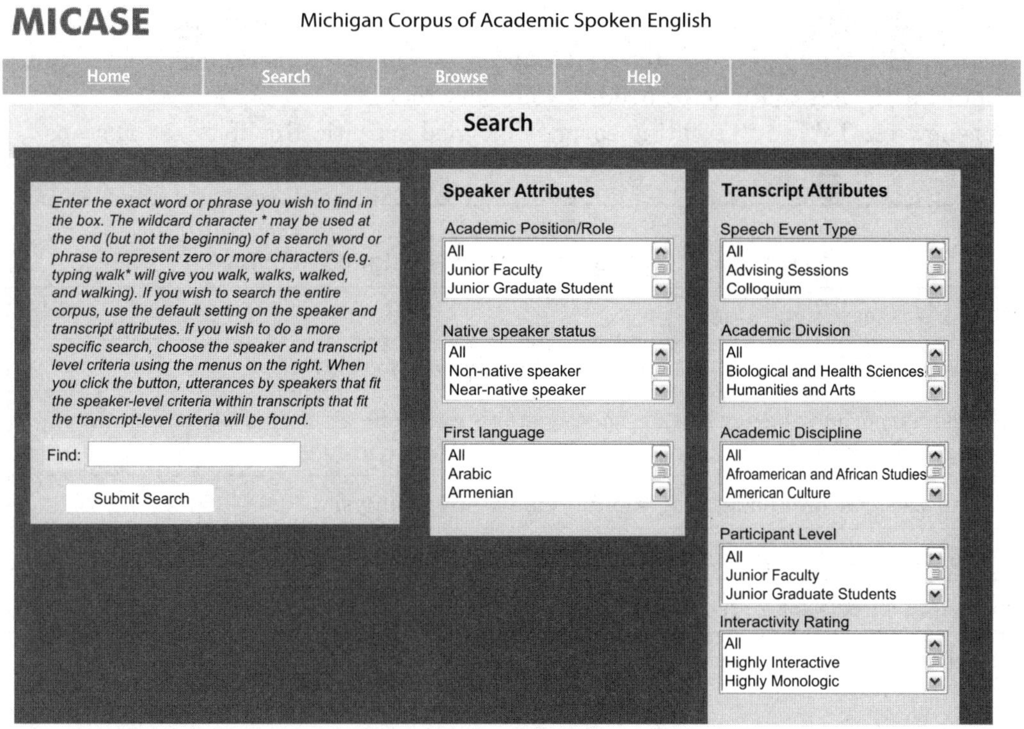

MICASE allows users to search for a word or phrase within the corpus. You can also narrow your search by specifying various speaker attributes or transcript attributes, so that the concordancing program will only display results of the word or phrase you are searching that are found within those attributes.

Source: http://micase.elicorpora.info. Used with permission.

An example of this type of basic concordancing program is TextSTAT 2.8 (Hüning, 2008). TextSTAT, Simple Text Analysis Tool, can be downloaded free from the Internet and has all the basic features needed to access a corpus:

> Download **TextSTAT** at http://neon.niederlandistik.fu-berlin.de/textstat/.

uploading of files to create a corpus, retrieving of word forms, viewing of concordance lines, and accessing of extended context. These basic features allow users to retrieve word frequencies from the corpus and sort alphabetically (or by frequency or by retrograde, alphabetically backward), to establish a minimum/maximum frequency, and to search for words containing affixes, as well as search and view concordance lines and extended context. WordSmith Tools (Scott, 2004) and MonoConc Pro (Barlow, 2007) are other concordancing programs that can be downloaded from the Internet. WordSmith Tools and MonoConc Pro do have a cost, but a personal license (for use on your personal computer) is affordable.

PROCEDURES

A Framework for Creating Corpus-Designed Activities

Parts 2 and 3 of this book focus on the applications of corpus linguistics to language teaching, with many of the chapters (Chapters 4–7) focusing specifically on corpus-designed activities that can be used in your classroom.

As shown in Table 1.2, creating corpus-designed activities involves seven steps.

Table 1.2
A Framework for Creating Corpus-Designed Activities

- Ask a research question.
- Determine the register on which your students are focused.
- Select a corpus appropriate for the register (or compile authentic texts from that register).
- Utilize a concordancing program for quantitative analysis.
- Engage in qualitative analysis.
- Create exercises for students.
- Engage students in a whole-language activity.

Ask a research question.

The "research question" for a corpus-designed activity could resemble, "What's the difference between *through* and *between*?" which was discussed earlier in this chapter. Or, "How do you use signal words in academic speaking?" which will be explored in Chapter 5.

Determine the register on which your students are focused.

As previously discussed, language is used differently in different registers. It's important when creating a corpus-designed activity that you know which register is relevant for your students. If students are practicing informal conversation, looking at a corpus of academic papers won't be helpful.

Select a corpus appropriate for the register (or compile authentic texts from that register).

Whether you create your own corpus or you use a corpus that already exists is not particularly relevant to creating a corpus-designed activity beyond the appropriate register and size of the corpus. What is important is that the corpus contains authentic language used for real-life communication.

Utilize a concordancing program for quantitative analysis.

Utilizing a concordancing program is the third step in the corpus approach. To create a corpus-designed activity, a concordancing program must be used to access the language stored in the corpus. If you are using a corpus that has a built-in concordancing program, be sure to understand all the search functions. If you are employing an outside concordancing program with a corpus, be sure that the program performs the functions you need to answer your research question.

Engage in qualitative analysis.

Qualitative analysis is the last step of the corpus approach. Most often, qualitative analysis will answer the question *Why?* For qualitative analysis, take the quantitative information given by the corpus's concordancing program and determine its significance.

Create exercises for students.

Preparing concordance lines and traditional fill-in-the-blank and gap-fill activities for students to examine and engage in is a central element of corpus-designed activities.

Engage students in a whole-language activity.

The grammar methodology of form, meaning, and use is also applicable to applying corpus linguistics in the classroom. The first and second steps of this methodology, form and meaning, are addressed through corpus-designed activities; but when applying corpus linguistics in the classroom, you should also ensure that students have an opportunity to use the target feature under investigation. Creating gap-fill exercises and whole-language activities will provide such opportunities for students and encourage acquisition of the target features at hand. Examples of these types of activities are included in Part 3.

Look again at the steps for creating corpus-designed activities listed in Table 1.2. What do you notice? The steps of the process are not numbered; this is because they may not take place specifically in this order. You may start with a research question, a corpus, a register, or even a whole language activity.

As you read Chapters 4–7, refer back to this framework for creating corpus-designed activities; it will help you make the connection from the reading and exercises to creating your own activities.

Modifying Activities by Language Level

Most of the activities discussed in Part 3 require at least an intermediate to high-intermediate level of English, but there are ways to modify corpus-designed activities to make them more accessible to your students. By their nature, corpus activities are for more advanced levels, but they can be adapted for students at lower levels.

To modify corpus-designed activities for low (beginning to low-intermediate) language level:

▶ Ask simple research questions.
▶ Find your own concordance lines.
▶ Adapt lines for students' level.
▶ Present students with fewer lines.
▶ Encourage group or whole class work.

Ask simple research questions.

General questions that have to do more with language as a whole are usually less ambiguous and more significant for lower-level students than specific questions like, "What's the difference between *through* and *between*?" For example, if you are teaching a group of Hispanic students who consistently use *have* to tell how old they are, a simple activity with *have* versus *am* when giving age can be very enlightening for learners.

Find your own concordance lines.

Instead of utilizing a whole corpus of authentic English for lower-level students to navigate, look for instances of the pattern you would like to investigate in materials around you, like the textbook, a newspaper, or magazine.

Adapt lines for students' level.

Materials that you intend to use in your corpus-designed activity can be modified for sentence structure and vocabulary so long as the feature under investigation remains intact. For example, these following sentences are used in the Chapter 5 materials on using *though* in academic speaking and exemplify the notion that *though* can be used to show a contrast in ideas.

> The two disciplines do not appear on the surface to have very much in common. Historically, though, anthropologists and epidemiologists have worked together for a very long period of time.

The sentence structure and vocabulary in these two sentences is quite advanced for low-intermediate learners, but they can be modified and still demonstrate *though* showing a contrast in ideas:

> The study of culture and the study of people's health do not seem similar, though they have been studied together for a very long time.

While some corpus linguists may argue against this method, I believe it's a realistic way for lower-level students to take advantage of the benefits of learning from corpus-designed activities and outweighs any drawbacks of working with adapted language.

Ask students to work with fewer lines.

Students don't necessarily have to study 20–50 lines in a corpus-designed activity; 10 lines may be enough for lower-level students to study, especially in investigations dealing with more general ideas, such as *have* versus *am,* as previously discussed.

Encourage group or whole class work.

Completing a corpus-designed activity as a whole class is another great way to give lower-level students exposure to the benefits of learning from corpus-designed activities without being too challenging for their language level.

ON YOUR OWN

For many instructors who want to provide the best possible instruction for their students but are pressed for time and resources, theoretical principles are often a luxury. What makes corpus linguistics work, so to speak, are the practical activities that can be used with students in an everyday classroom. Knowledge of what corpus linguistics is and is not, questions that corpora can answer, the corpus approach, types of corpora and concordancing programs, and how to create corpus-designed activities all help to provide a solid foundation for understanding the applications of corpus linguistics. Try these activities to get an idea of how you can apply corpora to your language learning classroom.

1. Go to www.collins.co.uk/corpus/CorpusSearch.aspx to view the top 100 collocations of a word or words.

2. Visit http://corpus.byu.edu/bnc/x.asp to view a side-by-side comparison of frequency and collocation in spoken versus written language.

PART 2

CORPORA IN LANGUAGE TEACHING

——————————————— Many teachers would agree with Sinclair's (2003) observation that ambiguity, variation, terminology, and incompleteness are the four most difficult areas of language teaching.

Pedagogical applications of corpus linguistics can be manifested in three levels, or tiers: corpus-influenced materials, corpus-cited texts, and corpus-designed activities. Different corpus researchers and corpus linguists refer to these three levels in different ways. Some use the terms *corpus-based* to refer to materials that are influenced by corpus findings; others use the term *corpus-informed* to refer to these materials. Still other corpus "experts" use *corpus-informed* and *corpus-based* to refer to methods for conducting corpus research and do not refer to classroom materials at all with these terms. In this text, I use the terms *corpus-influenced materials, corpus-cited texts,* and *corpus-designed activities;* these terms can be used separately from theoretical discussions of corpus linguistics to accurately represent how teachers can use corpora in the classroom.

> Three tiers of pedagogical applications of corpus linguistics:
> - Corpus-influenced materials
> - Corpus-cited texts
> - Corpus-designed activities

Corpus-influenced materials are textbooks and other materials whose presentations and/or activities are influenced by corpus findings. Corpus-cited texts are extensive grammar and vocabulary references, usually consulted by teachers, that specifically cite corpus findings. Corpus-designed activities are activities designed for students to manipulate actual corpus data.

The pedagogical applications of corpus linguistics can be classified like sources for a research paper. Primary sources are original materials that have not been filtered through interpretation; these are *corpus-designed activities,* looking directly at a corpus and the evidence it provides. Secondary sources are interpretations and evaluations of primary sources. Secondary sources are not evidence, but rather commentary on and discussion of evidence; these are *corpus-cited texts.* Corpus-cited texts do not provide all the data from the corpus itself, but compilations of the evidence from the corpus, organized and presented to the reader. Tertiary sources consist of information that is a distillation and collection of primary and secondary sources. Corpus-influenced materials contain information and activities collected from the secondary and primary sources (corpus-cited texts and corpus-designed activities). Corpus-influenced materials and corpus-cited texts are discussed in Part 2 in Chapters 2 and 3. Corpus-designed activities are discussed in-depth in Part 3 in Chapters 4–7.

Chapter 2

Corpus-Influenced Materials

Corpus-influenced materials, as the name suggests, are textbooks and other class-room materials featuring presentations and/or activities that are influenced by corpus findings. Corpus-influenced materials look like other materials used in the classroom, but the information contained within them is influenced by a corpus. Corpus-influenced materials are the most practical way to get information provided by corpora into the hands of learners.

Because corpus-influenced materials are influenced by language in use observed in a corpus, they provide a more accurate picture of language and are often more accurate than traditional (i.e., non–corpus influenced) materials. The writers who write corpus-influenced materials do not have to rely on their intuition alone when developing texts. By developing corpus-influenced materials, writers can couple the detailed knowledge of language—as it is actually used—provided by a corpus with their own expertise of designing language activities. For example, the question in Chapter 1 asked about the difference between *is not* (or *'s not*) and *isn't*: because our intuition doesn't provide us with an answer to this type of question, it's not an area of language that materials writers could normally include in a textbook. However, because *Touchstone* (McCarthy, McCarten, & Sandiford, 2005) is influenced by the Cambridge International Corpus of North American English, this fact of language is noted in a grammar section featuring yes-no questions and answers, giving students an additional piece of the "language use" puzzle (see Figure 2.1).

The five ways corpus-influenced materials are more beneficial to students are:

1. They are based on actual language use, providing a more accurate picture of the language.
2. Their examples, although they may be edited or adapted, are a reflection of authentic language.
3. Their syllabi are informed by frequency information, providing learners exposure to more useful language.

Figure 2.1
Touchstone 1 Addresses the Issue of Using *'s not v. isn't*

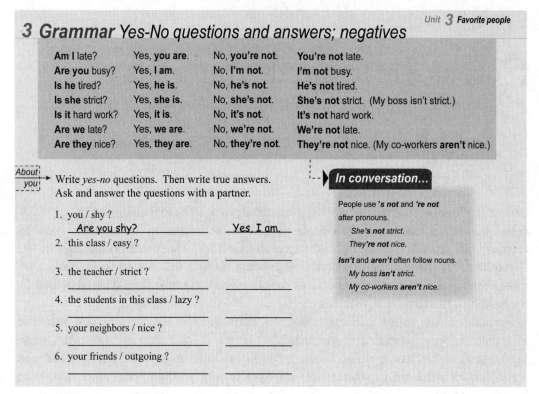

Source: *Touchstone 1*, Cambridge University Press, 2005.

4. They are able to distinguish how different language is used in different registers.

5. They can provide specialized language to particular groups of learners.

TARGET FEATURES

Although they appear the same in presentation as traditional classroom materials, corpus-influenced materials are distinguishable in a number of ways:

▪ Corpus-influenced materials can employ common lexical items in specific language patterns. For example, Thornbury (2004, p. 3) uses the lexical items *drink* and *look* for exercises dealing with *have a...* because these are among the most lexical items in this pattern in the British National Corpus (BNC).

- Corpus-influenced materials can provide the most common contexts for language patterns. For example, each chapter in Zwier (2002) focuses on a discourse meaning common in academic writing or spoken presentations and provides key vocabulary for that meaning. In Chapter 7, *stem from, yield, generate,* and *promote* are offered as key terms to describe cause and effect beyond connectives such as *as a result* and *because of* (Zwier, 2002, p. 145).

- Corpus-influenced materials can present targeted vocabulary according to frequency and saliency. For example, Azar (personal correspondence) focuses on the use of verbs such as *work, look, talk, go,* and *take* when presenting use of the perfect aspect.

Corpus-influenced materials offer additional advantages, as well. The most notable advantage to *Touchstone 1* (McCarthy, McCarten, & Sandiford, 2005), for example, is that the text is able to focus strongly on grammatical structures used in conversation, something not often present in other listening-speaking skills textbooks, which more traditionally emphasize vocabulary acquisition through discussion. Further, despite this concentration on grammatical structure, *Touchstone* also effectively incorporates the same vocabulary topics/words as do other speaking-listening texts, such as *Let's Talk* (Jones, 2001) and *NorthStar, Listening and Speaking* (2009), but with the added advantage of using the most frequent vocabulary found in conversation, such as noting that *like* is one of the top 15 words in conversation (McCarthy, McCarten, & Sandiford, 2005, p. 91).

> Vocabulary and grammar are often discussed in terms of frequency and saliency. **Frequency** is, of course, the raw counting of a word, phrase, or structure. A word, phrase, or structure that is salient may or may not be frequent. **Saliency** is assessed from being prominent or noticeable, regardless of frequency.

When students use textbooks that are influenced by real language use, both students and teachers have more confidence that the language learning is more targeted and maximized.

TOOLS

Some of the most notable examples of corpus-influenced materials for English language learning are listed organized by publisher.

Published Materials

Cambridge University Press (CUP)

Cambridge University Press authors have access to the CIC (see Appendix 1 for more information on this and other corpora), a 1 billion–word corpus of English, when writing materials. CUP has a special symbol to denote which of its publications are influenced by the CIC. Among them are

- ▶ *Touchstone* Series (basic through advanced integrated series)
- ▶ *Grammar in Use* Series (basic and intermediate grammar text)
- ▶ *Vocabulary in Use* Series (basic through upper-intermediate vocabulary text)
- ▶ *In the Know* (intermediate idioms text)

University of Michigan Press (UMP)

- ▶ *Building Academic Vocabulary* (advanced vocabulary text)
- ▶ *Academic Listening Strategies* (advanced academic listening text)
- ▶ *Academic Interactions* (advanced academic speaking text)
- ▶ *Academic Writing for Graduate Students* (graduate-level academic writing text)
- ▶ *Four Point* Series (high-intermediate and advanced integrated texts)
- ▶ *Thinking Beyond the Content* (advanced academic reading text)
- ▶ *Vocabulary Mastery* Series (low-intermediate through advanced vocabulary texts)
- ▶ *Teaching a Lexis-Based Academic Writing Course* (teacher resource for advanced writing and vocabulary)

Although UMP authors utilize a variety of corpora in materials writing—both *Building Academic Vocabulary* and *Teaching a Lexis-Based Academic Writing Course* are influenced by WordBanks Online, a 50 million–word corpus of modern English, and texts in the *Vocabulary Mastery* Series are influenced by the AWL (Coxhead, 2000)—many texts are influenced by the MICASE and future texts will be by MICUSP.

Oxford University Press

▶ *Natural Grammar* (intermediate to advanced grammar text) This is influenced by the BNC and focuses on grammatical patterns of the 100 most common words of English.

Heinle Cengage Learning

▶ *English for Academic Success* Series (low-intermediate to advanced oral communication, reading, writing, and vocabulary texts)

Texts in this series are influenced by a number of corpora, from WordBanks Online to the AWL.

Pearson Longman

▶ *Focus on Vocabulary* (high-intermediate vocabulary text)
▶ *Vocabulary Power* Series (low-intermediate through advanced vocabulary text)
▶ *Understanding and Using English Grammar* (high-intermediate grammar text)

Both *Focus on Vocabulary* and the *Vocabulary Power* Series are influenced by the AWL, while *Understanding and Using English Grammar* is influenced by the Longman Spoken American Corpus and the Longman Written American Corpus.

PROCEDURES

As with any classroom materials, corpus-influenced materials should be evaluated according to students' learning needs. The Checklist on page 30 can be useful in evaluating potential classroom materials. By nature, corpus-influenced materials will readily address several aspects of the Checklist, such as containing authentic texts and tasks, allowing for adaptability, and including both deductive and inductive activities to encourage noticing. The Checklist is followed by examples (Figures 2.2–2.5) that illustrate this point.

Materials Analysis Checklist

Grammar Materials	Reading Materials
• are logically sequenced. • exploit the three E's (explanations, examples, exercises) • provide grammar in context • utilize both inductive and deductive learning	• provide pre-, while-, and post-reading activities • contain appropriate text types and topics • use authentic texts, when possible • teach reading strategies
Speaking Materials	Writing Materials
• consider the appropriate audience • present grammar for the spoken context • address accuracy and fluency • address pronunciation • provide speaking strategies • link speaking and listening	• develop students' knowledge of rhetorical patterns • engage students in the writing process • provide opportunities for writing for both fluency and accuracy • connect reading and writing
Pronunciation Materials	
• focus on both segmentals and suprasegmentals	

Listening Materials
• include strategies for listening • allow for immediate post-listening production • provide pre-, while-, and post-listening activities • make use of appropriate spoken excerpts

Note: Special thanks to the members of the Graduate TESOL Cohort 03 and 04 in LIN 558 Materials Development and Integration in the M.A. TESOL program at Cornerstone University for helping to create this checklist in class.

Figure 2.2
This "Figure it out" Exercise in *Touchstone* Encourages Students to Notice the Past Tense

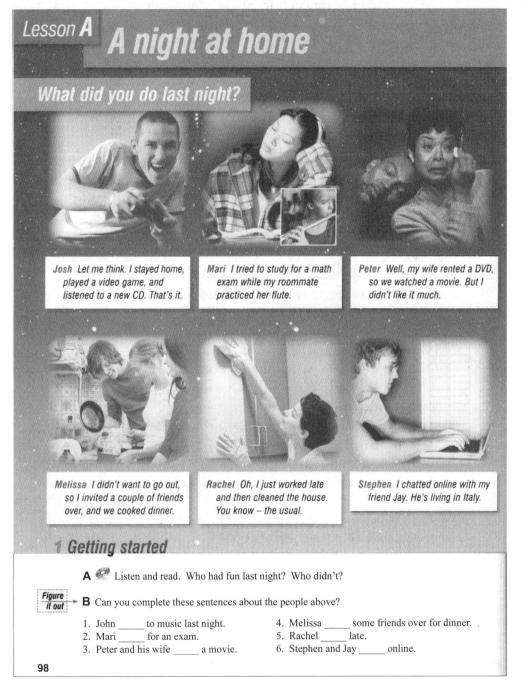

Lesson **A**
A night at home

What did you do last night?

Josh Let me think. I stayed home, played a video game, and listened to a new CD. That's it.

Mari I tried to study for a math exam while my roommate practiced her flute.

Peter Well, my wife rented a DVD, so we watched a movie. But I didn't like it much.

Melissa I didn't want to go out, so I invited a couple of friends over, and we cooked dinner.

Rachel Oh, I just worked late and then cleaned the house. You know – the usual.

Stephen I chatted online with my friend Jay. He's living in Italy.

1 Getting started

A Listen and read. Who had fun last night? Who didn't?

Figure it out

B Can you complete these sentences about the people above?

1. John _____ to music last night.
2. Mari _____ for an exam.
3. Peter and his wife _____ a movie.
4. Melissa _____ some friends over for dinner. .
5. Rachel _____ late.
6. Stephen and Jay _____ online.

98

Source: *Touchstone 1*, Cambridge University Press, 2005.

Figure 2.3
This "Writing Projects" Exercise in *Building Academic Vocabulary*
Allows Adaptability for Student Application

21 • Including, Making Up

📑 Writing Projects

1.11. Writing Projects. The following are some suggestions for writing projects that will allow you to use the key vocabulary and some of the additional vocabulary. Each of the topics could be lightly covered in an essay of 500–600 words or more thoroughly in a paper of 1,500–2,000 words. To write information-packed longer papers you should do some research in the library and/or on the Internet.

1. Analysts often try to group the nations of the world according to various schemes—for example, north vs. south, developed vs. developing, First World, Second World, Third World, etc. What do you think would be an effective and accurate system for classifying the nations of the world? Explain your system.
2. What is a family? Whom do you consider *your* family? On what do you base those beliefs? Write an essay about families and how to define them.
3. A modern city is an extremely complex combination of systems for delivering goods and services, transportation, electricity, waste disposal, food supply, etc. Think of a city you know well and describe it in terms of its essential systems. You could approach this topic in many different ways.
   Describing several systems and how they work together
   Describing a single system in great detail
   Comparing the systems in two or more cities
   Describing why some systems work well and others don't

Choose an approach that feels comfortable to you and follow it to produce an essay about the essential infrastructure of a city.

Source: *Building Academic Vocabulary*, the University of Michigan, 2002.

Figure 2.4
The "Collocations" Section in *Natural Grammar* Provides Lexical Items that Are Commonly Found in Certain Grammatical Patterns

place

[**countable noun**] a particular position or building, town, etc.:
Rio is a fantastic place. • *Come back to my place and have something to eat.* • *This is the place where I lost the ring.*
[**verb**] put: *Place the chicken in a large pot.*

Grammar patterns

1 its/my/her etc. + **place**

Put the books back in their place.
Julia's having a party at her place on Saturday.

▲ to talk about where something goes, or about where someone lives

2 a/an | (+ adjective) | + **place** | + to-infinitive

We're looking for a place to eat.
Where's the best place to buy shoes?

▲ to talk about where you do things

3 the | + **place** | (+ where/in which) | + clause

This is the place where I usually park the car.
You can visit the place in which Wordsworth wrote 'The Prelude.'
What's that place you went to last summer?

▲ to identify a place

Collocations

Place combines with a number of verbs:

If something *takes place*, it happens. (*The World Cup takes place every four years.*)
If you *take your place*, for example at a table, you go to the place chosen for you. If someone *takes the place of* someone, they replace them.
If you *get a place* on a team, or at a university, you become a member, student, etc.
If you *lose your place*, for example in a book, you don't know where you finished.
If someone *saves* or *keeps a place* for you, they guard it until you arrive. You can also *go back to your place*, and *change places* with someone.

The following adjectives and nouns frequently occur before place: *good, best, safe, right, wrong, nice, busy, quiet, strange, public, meeting, hiding,* and *market.*

The verb *place* is often followed by these nouns:
an order, an advertisement, a bet.

We placed an ad in the local paper.

The participle *placed* is often used after these adverbs:
well, ideally, uniquely, conveniently.

If you speak several languages you are well placed for a range of interesting jobs.

Set phrases

• **in place** = ready, or in the correct place
  Plans are in place for the development of the area.

• **in the first place**
  I don't understand why you chose to study archaeology in the first place.
  ▲ to talk about the beginning of a situation, especially to criticize it

• **all over the place** = in many different places, or in a state of disorder
  She travels all over the place as part of her job.

• **in his/her** etc. **place / in place of ...** = instead of
  For the sauce, you can use hazelnuts in place of almonds.

• **'(if I was/were) in your place...'**
  In your place, I'd get a lawyer.
  ▲ to give someone advice

• **'it's not my place to...'**
  It's not my place to criticize Aisha, but I think she's made the wrong choice.
  ▲ to say something that is not appropriate for you

• **out of place** = inappropriate or uncomfortable
  Doug's comments about John were out of place, I thought.
  He felt out of place at the party; all the other guests knew each other.

Source: *Natural Grammar*, Oxford University Press, 2004.

Figure 2.5
The Sentences in This Fill-in-the-Blank Exercise in *Teaching a Lexis-Based Academic Writing Course* **Use Authentic Texts for Each Word**

Chapter 8: Permitting, Making Easier

Quiz 3: Collocations and Common Phrases

I. Collocations and Common Phrases

Fill in each blank with the best item from the list. Not every item on the list will be used. Some items may be used more than once.

be	give	time
diagnosis	herself	treated
from	in	under
get	suffering	

1. The students prepared for the exams as throughly as _____ allowed.

2. A judge may refuse to accept a defendant's confession if it was obtained _____ circumstances where the police intimidated the suspect.

3. Children who are routinely excused _____ physical education classes do not get enough physical exercise.

4. In Tyrrhenian culture, mentally disabled criminals were _____ leniently because they were assumed to have no real understanding of their actions.

5. By signing this application, you _____ your consent for us to check your credit history.

6. Federal law says that medicine must _____ governmental approval before being marketed in the United States.

7. Negotiators from a few nations argued that, under the treaty, nuclear weapons should _____ exempt from international inspections.

<u>Source</u>: *Teaching a Lexis-Based Academic Writing Course*, the University of Michigan, 2006.

ON YOUR OWN

When using corpus-influenced materials in the classroom, instructors have reported that the focus on structure helps students feel more confident about communicating naturally in an English-speaking environment. Discussing the frequency and appropriateness with which American English speakers use language seems to satisfy students who often experience frustration at their inability to use "real" English outside the classroom. Students are pleased to learn structures that they can trust will occur frequently with native English speakers. As teachers often feel frustration in their intuitive attempts to provide students with relevant conversational phrases, corpus-influenced materials provides instructors with confidence to guide students in accurately using English that they are most likely to encounter all around them.

1. Consider Figures 2.2–2.5. How does each address collocation, lexicogrammar, register, and frequency?
2. Look at any of the textbooks listed on pages 28–29 that you have access to. How do they address collocation, lexicogrammar, register, and frequency? How do they measure up when analyzed with the Materials Checklist on page 30?

Chapter 3

Corpus-Cited Texts

Corpus-cited texts are extensive grammar and vocabulary references that specifically cite corpus findings. Authors of these references have conducted extensive research in extremely large, generalized corpora. Typically, corpus-cited texts are used by instructors to inform teaching; instructors consult corpus-cited texts to create lessons and/or supplement published teaching materials.

Corpus-cited texts can be thousands of pages long, and, therefore, appear quite intimidating. But don't be intimidated! The three major corpus-cited texts discussed here are well organized and provide helpful tools, such as conceptual as well as lexical indices and general as well as specific contents, to help the reader navigate the extensive amount of provided information. An important strategy to keep in mind when consulting corpus-cited texts is skimming. Reading word for word may be overwhelming and frustrating. Skimming the relevant sections for key words applicable to your lesson plan will be much more productive. Know what you want to research before you open those references.

TARGET FEATURES

There are several ways teachers can use corpus-cited texts to inform instruction. First, make sure published materials you are using provide pertinent information about the target language feature. Some grammar texts specify that the passive with *get* is inappropriate in formal writing and suggest its use only in spoken English. A search for the passive with *get* in the COCA, however, reveals that the structure is quite common in writing just as it is in speaking.

Corpus-cited texts can also add useful lexical details to a lesson. If you're teaching collective nouns, a corpus-cited text can provide more than the standard definition and examples, for example discuss with students how collective nouns are associated with a particular type of entity: people, animals, plants, or inanimate objects (Biber et al., 1999, p. 249). Explain that collective nouns are generally used for neutral descriptions, although some collective nouns can be used to express negative connotation, like *bunch, gang,* and *pack* (Biber et al., 1999, p. 249). Tell students that the most productive and useful collective nouns by far are *bunch of, group of,* and *set of* (Biber et al., 1999, p. 248). Concentrate practice activities around these examples.

Corpus-cited texts also provide important details about collocation. In addition to the knowledge that *bunch of, group of,* and *set of* are extremely productive collective nouns, and that *bunch of* can signify a negative meaning, provide facts about which words collocate with these collective nouns, offering students even more guidance on how to use language. Table 3.1, for example, shows the most common collocations for *bunch of, group of,* and *set of.*

Corpus-cited texts focus on grammar and vocabulary, but the information in corpus-cited texts is also organized according to register. This makes corpus-cited texts valuable to any instructor, regardless of the language skill being taught. For example, single adverbials are often used differently according to register. The single adverb *since* is used 95 percent of the time in academic prose to refer to "reason," but in conversation, fiction, and newspaper writing, *since* is used most commonly in reference to "time" (Biber et al., 1999, p. 846). Such distinctions can be extremely useful for language learners.

TOOLS

Teachers can take advantage of three major corpus-cited texts to inform their instruction: the *Longman Grammar of Spoken and Written English* (*LGSWE*) (Biber et al., 1999), the *Cambridge Grammar of English* (CGE) (Carter & McCarthy, 2006), and the *Oxford Collocations Dictionary* (OCD) (2002).

Longman Grammar of Spoken and Written English (LGSWE)

Using a 40 million–word corpus with four main registers—conversation, fiction, newspaper language, and academic prose—as its source, the *LGSWE* provides a descrip-

Table 3.1
Most Common Collocations of the Most Frequent Collective Nouns

bunch of	group of	set of
amateurs	adults	characteristics
idiots	friends	conditions
roses	girls	glasses

Source: *Oxford Collocations Dictionary for Students of English,* 2002.

tive and empirical assessment of language in use that demonstrates the interface of grammar, vocabulary, and choice; choices involve various facets such as reason for communicating, context, audience, and mode. The *LGSWE* provides details of how, taken together, these choices give rise to systematic patterns of English (Biber et al., 1999, p. 4).

A useful feature for teachers of the *LGSWE* is its empirical description of language. Informing students that more than half of the nouns in academic prose have a modifier (Biber et al., 1999, p. 578) adds a degree of certainty and confidence to students learning language that can't be gained any other way. An awareness that *oh* is the most common interjection in spoken American English is evidence that students can concretely examine (Biber et al., 1999, p. 1096). Also, the example and text extracts offered as examples in the *LGSWE* are drawn from authentic sources in the corpus, therefore providing students with real examples of language in use.

Cambridge Grammar of English (CGE)

Using the CIC as its source, the *CGE* presents probabilistic rules of grammar, meaning that the rules presented "state what is most likely or least likely to apply in particular circumstances" (Carter & McCarthy, 2006, p. 5). As you would expect in a corpus-cited text, the *CGE* provides a descriptive approach to grammar based on observation of usage; it illustrates how people actually use language. The authors stress that both grammar as structure and grammar as choice are treated in the *CGE*, and the grammar of choice is as important as the grammar of structure (Carter & McCarthy, 2006, p. 7). While learners don't have to mimic native speakers' language to be successful, it is important for learners to observe and understand how and why speakers use the language they do; describing language in use is not a prescription for learner use, but a presentation of data so that teachers and learners can make their own informed choices, a significant aspect of language learning (Carter & McCarthy, 2006, p. 10) that can only be addressed and developed with information from a corpus, in this case, presented in a corpus-cited text.

The *CGE* offers an extensive look at communicative functions of language use. In terms of frequency, the *CGE* only says that prepositional phrases are *extremely* common as post-modifiers—while the *LGSWE* tells us that 80 percent of post-modifiers are prepositional phrases (Biber et al., 1999, p. 606)—but the *CGE* continues to explain that prepositional phrases serving as post-modifiers act to identify the noun they are modifying in order to distinguish it from other nouns (Carter & McCarthy, 2006, pp. 327–328). For example, the prepositional phrase *in the plan* identifies "the proposals" in the sentence *The five main proposals in the plan were considered at yesterday's meeting* (Carter & McCarthy, 2006, p. 328). Students appreciate knowing not only how to use certain language features, but also knowing under what circumstances to use those language features.

Oxford Collocations Dictionary for Students of English (OCD)

The entries and collocations in the *OCD* were designed around three practical questions: Is this a typical use of language? Might a student of English want to express this idea? Would students look up this entry to find out how? (*Oxford Collocations Dictionary*, 2002, p. viii).

To address the first question, the BNC was used as the source for the *OCD*, so frequency of combinations and contexts was easily checked. Furthermore, the example sentences provided in the *OCD* were taken directly from the authentic texts comprising the corpus. To answer the second question, moderately formal language is represented in the dictionary, given that most users of the dictionary are likely to be composing an academic essay or other written work. To address the final question, the *OCD* is organized with adjective entries listing verb, adverb, and prepositional collocations; verb entries listing adverb and prepositional collocations, in addition to any extended phrases; and noun entries listing adjective and verb collocations, in addition to any extended phrases.

The *OCD* can prove particularly useful in writing instruction, particularly for students who have a sufficient understanding of the topic and a base of appropriate vocabulary, but who cannot express their meaning with precision. In an essay on the economy, for example, looking up the entry for *economy* in the *OCD* provides the user with a list of adjectives to be used with *economy* (*booming, healthy, depressed, flagging, weak*); verbs that can be used with *economy* as the object (*build, manage, regulate*); verbs that can be used with the subject *economy* (*develop, expand, stabilize, collapse*); and phrases in which *economy* is a key lexical item (*the size of the economy, an area of the economy, growth of the economy*) (*Oxford Collocations Dictionary*, 2002, p. 248), allowing the writer tools for more precise writing. The *OCD* can also provide details that students can apply in conversation and discussion; we look at an activity of this sort later in this chapter.

PROCEDURES

As an example, the process for using a corpus-cited reference for supplementing published classroom materials in a high-intermediate grammar class in an IEP might work as described here.

Most of the students in your class wish to attend an American college or university, but some of the students will be returning to their home countries after they complete the program. You are working with adverb clauses of time in Chapter 5 of *Understanding and Using English Grammar*, 3rd edition (Azar, 2002, pp. 70–72). A review of the presentation materials (Charts 5.1 and 5.2) provides you with information that looks similar to other information you've taught on adverbs of time (see Table 3.2). When you taught this course last session, the students didn't seem to have any trouble with the information or exercises provided.

Table 3.2
Key Ideas about Adverb Clauses of Time

Adverb clauses of time	
When the phone rang, the baby woke up. The baby woke up *when the phone rang.*	These examples have the same meaning. An adverb clause can come in front of the main clause or follow the main clause. Notice that a comma is used to separate the two clauses when the adverb clause comes first.

Common adverb clauses to show time relationships		
after*, before*, when, while / as, by the time, since, until / till, as soon as / once, as long as / so long as, whenever / every time, the first / last / next time	* *After* and *before* are commonly used in the following expressions:	
	shortly *after* ***a short time*** *after* ***a little while*** *after* ***not long*** *after* ***soon*** *after*	***shortly*** *before* ***a short time*** *before* ***a little while*** *before* ***not long*** *before*

<u>Source</u>: Azar, 2002, pp. 70–72.

The Corpus-Cited Text

Knowing that corpus-cited texts can make your teaching and materials more effective, you look at the copy of the *LGWSE* in the school's professional library. In the Conceptual Index, look up "adverbs of time." After a quick scan, you find "time" under "adverbial clause as circumstance adverbial." You turn to page 818 to the chapter on Adverbials and begin to skim the information. You note that time clauses are very common in fiction and news (Biber et al., 1999, p. 820). You continue skimming through the discussion of the distribution across registers and the discussion of distribution of clausal syntactic forms (like *-ing* clause, *to* clause, etc.). Next, you notice the subsection dealing with positions of adverbial clauses (Biber et al., 1999, p. 830). This doesn't peak much interest because, as Azar (2002, p. 70) shows, adverb clauses of time can come at the beginning of a sentence, followed by a comma, or at the end of a sentence without a change in meaning. You notice a chart, though, that shows an overwhelming preference of adverbial clauses for final position. As you look more closely, you discover this: "Time clauses in all registers have a preference for final position, but the preference is stronger in the written register" (Biber et al., 1999, p. 833). This is very interesting! You make a note to mention to your students that, while adverb clauses can come at the beginning or end of a sentence

Figure 3.1
Most Common Time Adverbial Subordinators across Register

Most common circumstance adverbial subordinators across registers and dialects; occurrences per million words

each ■ represents 200   □ represents less than 100

	CONV (AmE & BrE)	FICT	NEWS (AmE & BrE)	ACAD
time				
when	■■■■■■■■ ·■■	■■■■■■■ ■	■■■■■■■ ■■	■■■■
as	■	■■■■■	■■	□
after	■	■■	■■■■	■
before	■	■■■	■■	■
while	■	■■■	■■	□
until	■	■	■	■
since	■	■	■	□

Source: Biber et al., 1999, p. 842.

without a change in meaning, adverb clauses dealing with time are mostly found at the end of a sentence, especially in writing. Students who want to attend university and those who will be returning to their home countries will find this information useful.

You continue scanning the information and find a chart presenting the most common "time" subordinator across registers. Overwhelmingly, *when* is the most frequent subordinator for adverbial clauses of time in all registers (Biber et al., 1999, p. 842) (see Figure 3.1). In fact, no other single subordinator is used very frequently at all in conversation. The results are even more striking for academic writing! The second most used subordinator overall is *as*, particularly in fiction. You must tell your students of the productive and overwhelming use of *when* in adverbial clauses of time.

As you continue skimming the chapter on Adverbials, you come to a section about subordinators that have multiple semantic roles (see Figure 3.2). You find that *since* is used to express "reason" and "time." Conversation and news more commonly use *since* to express time (about 75 percent), but academic prose rarely uses *since* in adverbial clauses of time; in fact, *since* expresses time less than 5 percent in academic prose (Biber et al., 1999, p. 846). You also find that *while* is used only 10 percent of the time to express "time" in academic writing, but *while* is used more than 95 percent of the time in conversation to express "time" (Biber et al., 1999, p. 849). You certainly want to tell your students that *since* and *while* are not productive for use with an adverbial clause of time in academic prose, but are extremely so in conversation.

Figure 3.2
Proportional Breakdown of Semantic Categories for the Subordinators *as* and *since* across Dialects and Registers

Proportional breakdown of semantic categories for the subordinator *as* across dialects and registers

each ■ represents 5%   □ represents less than 2.5%

	manner	reason	time
AmE CONV	■■■■■■■■■■■	□	■■■■■■■■■
BrE CONV	■■■■■■■■■■■■	■■	■■■■■■
FICT	■■■■■■■	■	■■■■■■■■■■■■■
AmE NEWS	■■■■■■■■	□	■■■■■■■■■■■■
BrE NEWS	■■■■	■	■■■■■■■■■■■■■■■ ■■
ACAD	■■■■■■■■■■■■■■	■■	■■■■■

Proportional breakdown of semantic categories for the subordinator *since* across dialects and registers

each ● represents 5%

	reason	time
AmE CONV	●●●●●	●●●●●●●●●●●●●●●●
BrE CONV	●●●	●●●●●●●●●●●●●●●●●●
FICT	●●●●●●●●●●●●	●●●●●●●●
AmE NEWS	●●●●●	●●●●●●●●●●●●●●●
BrE NEWS	●●●●●●	●●●●●●●●●●●●●
ACAD	●●●●●●●●●●●●●●●●●●●●	●

Source: Biber et al., 1999, pp. 847–848.

Application

Looking at the corpus-cited text to supplement your lesson planning led to the discovery of three very important pieces of additional information to share with students when teaching adverb clauses of time:

1. Adverb clauses of time mostly come at the end of a sentence, especially in writing.
2. *When* is, by far, the most common subordinator used in adverb clauses of time, in all registers.
3. *Since* and *while* are not normally used as adverb clauses of time in academic prose, but are especially common as adverb clauses of time in conversation.

Providing your students with these additional facts about adverb clauses of time will certainly allow for a more meaningful and useful lesson on the subject.

As another example, the process for using a corpus-cited reference for supplementing materials in a listening-speaking class using the textbook *Talk It Over! 3* (Kozyrev, 2002) follows.

The current chapter focuses on the topic of "family." One of the final exercises deals with preparing for and participating in a discussion. The provided discussion questions include making comparisons about your family and childhood, evaluating the idea of privacy, and discussing children traveling (see Figure 3.3). Family is a familiar topic, so you feel confident that students will not have a problem with content; however, you'd like to offer students a concrete language feature they can practice during the free discussion.

For the key ideas in each question—childhood, privacy, and traveling—you prepare a list of useful collocations from the *Oxford Collocations Dictionary for Students of English* (2002) that students can apply to a discussion of these topics and provide students with the tables on page 44. When reviewing the charts in class, you point out and discuss the connotations that seem to accompany each word:

- *Childhood* collocates with more negative words (e.g., *difficult, traumatic, survive, disease*); does this mean when people discuss childhood the conversation is usually more negative?

- A sense of control is present in the collocates for *privacy*? What does this tell you about how people feel about their privacy?

- Not surprisingly, the prepositions that collocate with *travel* signify place. What surprises you about the verbs, including phrases, that collocate with *travel*? Do you feel people experience a sort of longing to travel?

Figure 3.3
Excerpt from *Talk It Over! 3*

Discussion Questions

1. How is your family and childhood different from or similar to your parents' families and childhoods? If you have or plan to have children, how will their experiences be different from yours?

2. Carol Berkin says that privacy was not valued in colonial times, and Jay Neugeboran says that "privacy is a wonderful thing." Is privacy something that you value highly? Can privacy ever be a bad thing?

3. Jay Neugeboren's children traveled to different places at young ages, but he did not. How far from home do you think colonial children got to travel? Is it important for children to see different places and to travel? How does travel affect your understanding of the world?

Source: From *Talk It Over! 3*, Heinle Cengage, p. 15.

Table 3.3
Collocations for Use with *childhood*

Adjectives	Verb + *childhood*	*childhood* + noun	Preposition + *childhood*
happy, difficult, lonely, normal, deprived, traumatic	*have, spend, survive*	*years, experiences, memories, friend, disease, illness*	*during, from, in, throughout*

Source: *Oxford Collocations Dictionary for Students of English,* 2002, p. 115.

Table 3.4
Collocations for Use with *privacy*

Adjectives	Verb + *privacy*	*privacy* + preposition	Phrases
complete, total, personal	*preserve, protect, respect, disturb, intrude on, invade, violate*	*from*	*in the* privacy *of, an* invasion *of* privacy

Source: *Oxford Collocations Dictionary for Students of English,* 2002, p. 595.

Table 3.5
Collocations for Use with *travel[ing]*

Verb + *travel*	*travel* + preposition	Phrases
be able / unable to, be free to, want to, wish to, have to	*across, along, around, between, from, through, to*	*freedom to* travel, *go* traveling, travel *light*

Source: *Oxford Collocations Dictionary for Students of English,* 2002, p. 822.

Providing supplemental facts about language, such as collocations for discussion topics, can offer students a more concrete way to develop not only their discussion skills, but to also develop an understanding of the cultural senses of topics.

ON YOUR OWN

Corpus-cited texts provide a plethora of valuable details about language that can help students more confidently, and perhaps more quickly, become expert users of the language. As busy, yet caring, teachers, our time is limited and valuable. We do all we are able to provide the best instruction to our students; taking advantage of the information provided in corpus-cited texts to create and/or supplement classroom materials is one of the most effective actions that a teacher can take for his or her students.

1. To determine if you should consult a corpus-cited text for your lesson planning, examine the textbook you are using to see if it addresses the areas listed. If it does not, you probably need to consult a corpus-cited text.

   a. frequency
   b. register
   c. context
   d. phraseology

PART 3

CORPUS-DESIGNED ACTIVITIES

——————————————— Part 3 discusses activities that implement the final tier of using corpora in the classroom, corpus-designed activities.

Corpus-designed activities are activities where students manipulate actual corpus data. Corpus-designed activities have their roots in Data-Driven Learning (DDL). DDL was developed almost two decades ago at the University of Birmingham, England, by Tim Johns (Johns, 1997). Johns developed DDL because findings in corpus linguistics are too important to be handled only by researchers (Johns, 1997). In DDL, students serve as "language detectives," asking questions and discovering facts about language themselves from authentic examples (Johns, 1997). In completing corpus-designed activities, students will engage in what Carter and McCarthy (1995) term the "three Is:" illustration—looking at real data; interaction—discussing and sharing opinions and observations; and induction—making one's own rule for a particular linguistic feature.

A **node** can be a single word (*however*), a lemma (*go, goes, going, went, gone*), a phrase (*I don't want…*), or a frame (*is…to*).

Other than a simple list of words from a corpus, concordance lines, all the instances of a word or phrase (called the *node*) in a corpus with minimal surrounding text, are the most common way of manipulating corpus data.

Chapters 4–7 present four corpus-designed activities using concordance lines to demonstrate the use of corpora in the classroom. The chapters provide guidance in designing additional activities. The included activities were among the first corpus-designed activities I used in my own classroom, and, therefore, seemed ideal to use in presenting corpus-designed activities to novice corpus users. The specificities of the activities—the language function and register—were defined according to the context of the original classroom I was teaching in when I designed the activities. Following the framework given for creating corpus-designed activities and understanding the process behind the designed activities will enable teachers to create corpus-designed activities for their own individual instructional setting. Readers may find it useful to refer to the Procedures section of Chapter 1 (pages 18–20) where the framework of creating corpus-designed activities is discussed.

Chapter 4

"I never noticed that before!" Patterns for *a/an* and *the* in Televised News Shows

The corpus-designed activity described in this chapter stems from two steps in the framework (see page 18): a whole-language activity and a register. This activity was created for a high-intermediate non-academic course focusing on media, as preparatory work for students' final project. Students studied 40 sentences from the spoken subcorpus of the COCA (Davies, 2008) to identify the patterns of *a* and *the* used in the corpus.[1] Students then completed a gap-fill activity, followed by application of the *a* and *the* patterns in their own projects.

TARGET FEATURE: ARTICLES

Indefinite and definite articles are one of the most challenging features of English for learners. Their ubiquity, coupled with the fact that many Indo-European, Slavic, Baltic, and Asian languages do not have articles, challenges even the most advanced English language learners. Given this, *a* and *the* were chosen as the focus of this corpus-designed activity.

The articles *a* and *the* are the most common determiners, a group of words that refer to a noun. Key ideas about the use of articles in English (Biber et al., 1999, pp. 260–269) follow:

▶ *a/an* is used with singular countable nouns, often to introduce a new, specific noun into discourse or to refer to any general noun or classify a noun

▶ *the* is used with both singular and plural countable and non-countable nouns, to refer to a known or understood noun

---

1. Why was studying *a* and *the* important? It wasn't, really, at the outset. I just wanted to see if I could come up with something corpus related; since we had to focus on media, I tried the news route. I actually started with a collection of about five newspaper articles and made a word list. I was studying the word list trying to come up with something interesting I could present in class. I noticed that *a/the* were among the top of the word list frequency. It wasn't surprising, but I wanted to check it out. I looked at lines from the small newspaper corpus I had (the five articles) and noticed the patterns. I went to the COCA to follow up. It was interesting, and I knew that advanced learners needed help with articles, and it fit nicely into the corpus, so that's why I did it. That's how the activity was born.

▶ *the* is more common than *a/an* in all registers (conversation, fiction, news, and academic prose)

▶ 80–85 percent of articles in the subject position are *the*, while *a/an* and *the* are split about 50 percent each in the object position.

Furthermore, as exemplified in the concordance lines from the COCA, *the* is often used in the pattern *the* + (proper) noun, and *a* is often used in the pattern *a* + adjective + noun.

TOOLS

For this corpus-designed activity, a class can read and discuss newspapers as well as watch news broadcasts over the course of several class periods. This exposure enables students to "model" what they learn from the authentic materials in their own projects, but the addition of a corpus-designed activity such as this one can help students focus on discrete language items while still engaging in communicative language practices.

The COCA is a large generalized corpus of American English freely available on the Internet. At the time of publication, the COCA contained more than 385 million words divided among transcripts of spoken language, fiction, popular magazines, newspapers, and academic texts. The spoken subcorpus alone contains more than 78 million words from televised news broadcasts and talk shows such as ABC's *20/20* and *Primetime* and CNN's *Larry King Live* and *Crossfire*.

Visit **COCA** on the web: www.americancorpus.org/.

The COCA has an excellent built-in concordancer that allows users to search for words, phrases, lemmas, parts of speech, and frames, among others. You can search the entire corpus, or search according to register. A unique and useful function of the COCA concordancer is the ability to compare results for two registers side by side (see Figure 4.1).

You may view as many lines from the corpus as you'd like (there are more than 1,000 pages of concordance lines for *the* in the spoken subcorpus!), but you may also chose a random sample of 100 entries. The lines created for this activity were taken from a sample of 100 lines. Figure 4.2 shows the search for *the* in the spoken subcorpus. Figure 4.3 shows the KWIC (Key Word in Context), or concordance, lines for *the*. Like most concordancers, you can also view extended context for the node (see Figure 4.4).

Frequency counts and concordance lines for this type of activity can be obtained by entering the node(s) into the COCA concordancer, in this case the words *the* and *a*[2]

---

2. The COCA contains a useful five-minute guided tour that details the major features of the corpus and concordancer. Query language, such as enclosing a word in brackets—as in [be]—to find all forms of a word or using an asterisk—*—to denote a variable word, are explained in the guided tour.

Figure 4.1
Comparing a Node in Two Subcorpora of the Corpus

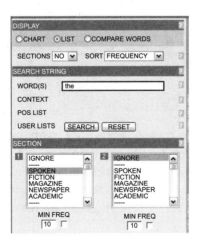

DISPLAY			?
○CHART ⊙LIST ○COMPARE WORDS			
SECTIONS [NO ▾] SORT [RELEVANCE ▾]		?	

SEARCH STRING		?
WORD(S) [the]	?	
CONTEXT	?	
POS LIST	?	
USER LISTS [SEARCH] [RESET]	?	

SECTION		?

1 | IGNORE

SPOKEN
FICTION
MAGAZINE
NEWSPAPER
ACADEMIC
------

2 | IGNORE

SPOKEN
FICTION
MAGAZINE
NEWSPAPER
ACADEMIC

MIN FREQ
[10] ☑

MIN FREQ
[10] ☐

SEE CONTEXT: CLICK ON WORD (ALL SECTIONS) OR NUMBER (SPECIFIED SECTION)   [HELP...]

SEC 1: 78,819,050 WORDS

	WORD/PHRASE	TOKENS 1	TOKENS 2	PM 1	PM 2	RATIO
1	THE	3746584	4998124	47,533.99	65,600.35	0.72

SEC 2: 76,190,503 WORDS

	WORD/PHRASE	TOKENS 2	TOKENS 1	PM 2	PM 1	RATIO
1	THE	4998124	3746584	65,600.35	47,533.99	1.38

Source: COCA.

Figure 4.2
Node *the* with the Option to View Results from the Spoken Subcorpus

DISPLAY	?
○CHART ⊙LIST ○COMPARE WORDS	
SECTIONS [NO ▾] SORT [FREQUENCY ▾]	?

SEARCH STRING	?
WORD(S) [the]	?
CONTEXT	?
POS LIST	?
USER LISTS [SEARCH] [RESET]	?

SECTION	?

1 | IGNORE

SPOKEN
FICTION
MAGAZINE
NEWSPAPER
ACADEMIC
------

2 | IGNORE

SPOKEN
FICTION
MAGAZINE
NEWSPAPER
ACADEMIC

MIN FREQ
[10] ☐

MIN FREQ
[10] ☐

Source: COCA.

Figure 4.3
Sample Entries for *the* in the Spoken Subcorpus of the COCA

KEYWORD IN CONTEXT (KWIC)				More Information...
CLICK ON TITLE FOR MORE CONTEXT			PAGE: « < 1/1000 > »	
SECTION: SPOKEN			SAMPLE: 100 ENTRIES	
1	1990 SPOK ABC_2020	I'm Barbara Walters. And this is 20/20. From ABC News, around the world and into your home, the stories that touch your life. With Hu
2	1990 SPOK ABC_2020	is 20/20. From ABC News, around the world and into your home, the stories that touch your life. With Hugh Downs and Barabara Walters
3	1990 SPOK ABC_2020	his wife. And I jumped up and I said, "What in the devil are you doing?" I thought, "Oh, my God
4	1990 SPOK ABC_2020	her." It has happened. John Stossel reports experts call sleepwalking. "The Twilight States." And Roger Caras asks, if something happe
5	1990 SPOK ABC_2020	him everything, will he land in heaven or flound in legal limbo? The animals are really victims. They really become victims themselve
6	1990 SPOK ABC_2020	I felt that I was evil. Did he do it? That's the question, after this total transformation. Lynn Sherr with a mysterious case and a
7	1990 SPOK ABC_2020	to a startling revelation. Well, this is a man who says that the best days of his life have been his years on Death Row. This is
8	1990 SPOK ABC_2020	could have been found guilty of such a horrible double murder. Lynn Sherr has the story of Joe Giarratano and his growing number of f

Users can click on the entry to view specific source information as well as extended context for each line. The first column on the left displays the number of the concordance line. The second left column shows the date of the concordance line. The column third from the left shows the subcorpus that the concordance is taken from. The second column from the right shows the source of the concordance line, and the far right column is the concordance line.

Source: COCA.

Figure 4.4
Extended Context for a Concordance line

EXPANDED CONTEXT		More information
Source information:		
Date	2009 (090127)	
Title	STEALING AT AN OPEN HOUSE; STICKY FINGERS	
Source	ABC_Primetime	

Expanded context:

Georgia Mason is a professor and Canada Research Chair in Animal Welfare at the University of Guelph in Ontario. And Paul Boyle is a senior vice president for conservation and education at the Association of Zoos and Aquariums in Silver Spring, Maryland. Thanks to both of you. Dr-BOYLE: Thanks, Joe. Dr-MASON: Thanks.' 256486 CONTENT: OPEN HOUSE JOHN-QUINONES-1-A# Off-camera You might think what houses are selling for these days is a steal. But the real steal is what's going on at the open houses, where sticky fingers can lead to a sticky situation. JOHN-QUINONES-1-A# Voiceover In a suburb of New Jersey, this $1.4 million home is up for sale, and this weekend, there's an open house to help bring in prospective buyers. ACTRESS-1FEMALE2# Hi, nice to meet you. PROSPECTIVE-BUYER-# Hi. JOHN-QUINONES-1-A# Voiceover While most folks have come to check out the cabinets and details of the house, something strange is going on

Source: COCA.

(as shown in Figure 4.2). Upon review of the data, register, and other patterns of the node, such as those mentioned, will become apparent. Frequency information and concordance lines that will be used in the actual activity should be adapted from the lines provided by the concordancer. Please be sure, too, that any handouts you make from material using the COCA lists COCA as the source of the information.

PROCEDURES

To begin this corpus-designed activity, engage students in a discussion about articles, including students' current understanding of use. Discuss the frequencies presented in Table 4.2. If students have not ever been introduced to a corpus or concordancing tools or have not analyzed language from an empirical perspective, they are typically extremely interested in (and impressed with!) the information. Observing the empirical data from the COCA can also establish a sort of trust with students; knowing that the information they are presented is taken from actual language used makes the students more engaged in the learning and application process.

After general discussion about articles, copies of the 20 concordance lines each for *a* and *the* can be distributed (see Appendix 2A). Although students may be extremely interested in the statistics from the corpus, they might, understandably, be quite overwhelmed by the 40 lines in front of them. It won't take long for students to get comfortable working with the concordance lines, especially once you walk them through the first couple of steps. That process should go something like this:

▶ Look at the first concordance line: *You need to take a hard look at it.*

▶ Highlight the word *a* in the first line: *You need to take a hard look at it.*

▶ Underline two words to the right of *a*: *You need to take a hard look at it.*

▶ Highlight *a,* and underline two words to the right of *a* in the rest of the items (as in Figure 4.5).

▶ What do the underlined words in the sentences have in common?

Lead the students to draw the conclusion that, in most cases, an adjective and a noun follow *a*. Display the pattern on the board:

a + adjective + noun

After working through the *a* concordance lines, pass out copies of the *the* concordance lines (see Appendix 2A), and ask students to repeat the same procedures, as shown in Figure 4.6.

Table 4.1
Frequency Information per million for *the* and *a* in the COCA (Davies, 2008)

Subcorpus	a/an	the
Spoken	24,674	47,534
Fiction	25,630	53,399
Magazine	28,323	54,646
Newspaper	27,708	53,978
Academic	23,166	65,600

Figure 4.5
a **and Two Words to the Right**

---

1 *a puzzling personality.*
2 *a brutal double murder.*
3 *a different person.*
4 *A convicted killer proclaims he's innocent.*
5 *a good idea.*
6 *a handgun.*
7 *a fuel surcharge.*
8 *a restaurant, had his own cologne, and even starred in a music video.*
9 *a spray-on can?*
10 *a certain disappointment because I had hoped for more in my discussions with the Foreign Minister.*
11 *a prolonged deployment in an inhospitable region.*
12 *a sensible foreign policy.*
13 *a big splash now, but some industry analysts are wondering what will happen next.*
14 *a hard time.*
15 *a product that does so much harm?*
16 *A ship loaded with Indian refugees from Kuwait arrived in Dubai today.*
17 *a whole box.*
18 *a little bit about the savings and loan crisis.*
19 *a better idea to lie to Congress.*

Ask the students again what the underlined words in the sentences have in common, and lead them to the conclusion that, in many cases, a proper noun follows *the*; display the pattern on the board:

the + proper noun

In both cases, students may note that all concordance lines do not follow the mentioned patterns; this is, in fact, an excellent observation! As language in use is always changing and may vary from user to user and/or instance to instance, it will not always follow established patterns, instead occurring in "preferred" patterns (as discussed in Chapter 3 in reference to Carter & McCarthy, 2006). Encourage students to understand and accept the ambiguity of language in use.

Once students discover and understand the patterns related to the target feature, a gap-fill exercise is appropriate to engage students in form, meaning, and use of the target feature. The gap-fill exercise for this specific activity that can be distributed is in Appendix 2A.

For a similar activity, the creation of such a gap-fill exercise is relatively simple: Using the original concordance lines for each targeted feature, choose lines at an appropriate level and that have a straightforward display of the target features (that

Figure 4.6
***the* and Two Words to the Right**

1 *the President fearing* the reaction of markets to such a speech.
2 *the Nuremberg trials.*
3 *the Air Force* intelligence has it, obviously.
4 *the Taj Mahal* in Atlantic City.
5 *the rate of* growth of Medicare.
6 *the IRS.*
7 *the space shuttle* Columbia.
8 *the Soviets have* agreed to build at least ten commercial ships for Pepsi.
9 *The fact* that this is a very bad time for Americans can't be ignored.
10 *the U.N. resolution,* there has to be some reference to its content.
11 *the Europeans, who* think we are going to start a war immediately.
12 *the United States* generally or the current administration in particular.
13 *The Sierra Club* has split ranks with Earth.
14 *The City of Norwalk* contributes $3 million a year to the operating budget.
15 *the Persian Gulf* are doing the same.
16 *the Middle East* was inevitable.
17 *the State Department.*
18 *the late Robert F. Kennedy,* married Andrew Cuomo.
19 *the fastest finishing* horse in the *Derby field.*
20 *the Bundy cases.*

is, show the patterns discovered) (but the lines should be different from those used in the discovery exercise), delete the targeted feature from the lines, and then randomly mix them. Students can practice the meanings and patterns they just learned by filling in the appropriate target features.

Don't forget the importance of engaging students in a whole language exercise. Applying what the students have discovered is as important as the discovery itself.

> A traditional **pre/post-assessment** of students' use of the target features is an effective way to document progress when engaging students in corpus-designed activities. Post assessments could occur both immediately after the corpus-designed activity (such as during the Whole Language Activity) as well as after a period of time (such as at the end of the term during a student's final presentation).

ON YOUR OWN

This activity was designed for use in my advanced-level multi-skill class with a media theme. The odds of many instructors finding themselves in this same teaching situation are probably small. Almost every instructor, however, finds himself needing to focus on grammar in his classroom at some point. A corpus-designed activity like this one can be applied in any situation. Following the framework (see page 18) for creating corpus-designed activities can help any instructor create such an activity.

Because of my individual instructional setting, I began with the "determine on which register your students are focused." In my case, this was media. In your case, it may be academic writing. You may have a specific research question like, "How are linking adverbials used in academic writing?" In that case, your research question is set. In my case, however, I had to determine what area of language I wanted to investigate.

We began with a whole language activity and register (news). We then used the COCA to gather data for the activity. After we engaged in quantitative (analyzing the statistics from the corpus) and qualitative (analyzing the concordance lines) analysis, we created exercises for students, both discovery (analyzing the concordance lines) and form/meaning (gap-fill activity), and came full circle to engage students in the whole language activity. At the end of the class, students understood that the patterns they discovered through the corpus-designed activity wouldn't apply in every speaking or writing situation they encountered. They did, however, feel a soaring sense of confidence knowing that they would be able to correctly use articles in their assignment for this class.

This same activity could be expanded, however, to focus more generally on article usage, as in a high-intermediate or advanced grammar class. Combine the information given here for article usage in the spoken subcorpus with information about article usage in the other subcorpora. Build on the frequency figures given for individual subcorpora in Table 4.2, and select concordance lines from each of the subcorpora for *a* and *the*. You might have students work with all the *the* concordance lines in one class session and the *a* concordance lines in another class session, focusing on the differences between the articles. You could, alternatively, focus on *a* and *the* from one register in one class session and other registers in subsequent classes, focusing on different uses among registers. This corpus-designed activity could also be modified specifically for a writing class, using concordance lines from an academic writing corpus.

Any way you choose to implement such a corpus-designed activity into your classroom, students will appreciate the opportunity to discover and apply concrete patterns and information about previously "unattainable" language features.

1. Visit MICUSP at http://micusp.elicorpora.info. Using the Framework for Creating Corpus-Designed Activities found in Table 1.2 on page 18, design an activity with linking adverbials in academic writing. As an example, Figure 4.7 displays four uses of *however* that can be found in MICUSP.

Figure 4.7
Screenshot MICUSP Simple BETA Version:
The Linking Adverbial *however* Shown in Context

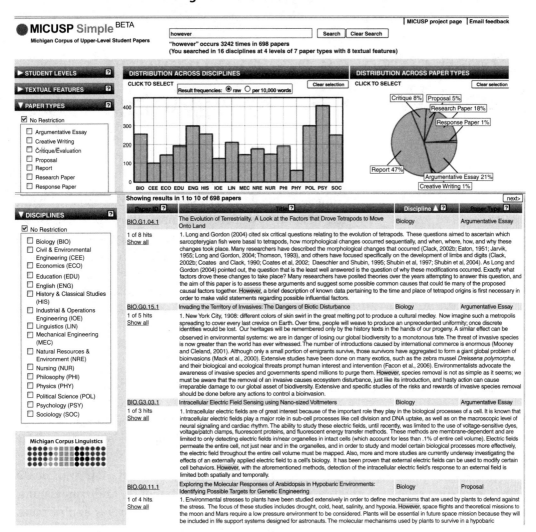

Source: http://micusp.elicorpora.info. Used with permission.

Chapter 5

"These patterns are eye opening."
Signal Words in Academic Speaking

The production skills of listening and speaking are sometimes the most difficult for students to master. They are also often difficult for instructors to teach. In an academic setting, specifically at a community college or university, some listening and speaking tasks can be crucial for student success. One such example is oral presentations. Many IEPs offer courses tailored to this specific need, and many textbooks addressing this subject are also available. One language feature these courses and textbooks generally discuss is linking adverbials, often referred to in listening/speaking lingo as **signal words**.

TARGET FEATURE: SIGNAL WORDS

Signal words are one of the most common linguistic features used in speaking. In conversation, signal words are only slightly less common than lexical verbs such as *run* and *eat*.

Because signal words allow speakers to mark the developments of their arguments and information, showing relationships, contrasts, restatements, and conclusions, they have more local functions in that they connect clauses to phrases and phrases to phrases, as opposed to global ideas such as paragraph to paragraph (Biber et al., 1999, pp. 875–880). The main function of signal words, though, is to state the speaker's perception of the relationship between two units of discourse to create textual cohesion (Biber et al., 1999, p. 875). In simpler terms, to provide a road map for what the speaker is saying.

In conversation, the most common signal words are *so* (used 3,400 times per million words), *then* (used 900 times per million words), and *though* (used 600 times per million words).

The activities that will be presented highlight the following features of these signal words:

▶ *So* is used to tell how one point or idea moves to another point or idea.

▶ *So* is followed by an independent clause (complete sentence).

▶ *So* is preceded by an independent clause (complete sentence).

▶ *So* frequently occurs in sentence medial position when functioning as a linking adverbial.

▶ *So* frequently occurs directly following *and*, a comma, or a period.

▶ *Then* is used to indicate addition, often to list items or events.

▶ *Then* is used mainly in sentence medial position.

▶ *Then* most frequently occurs in front of a verb phrase or independent clause.

▶ *Though* is used to mark a contrast.

▶ *Though* most frequently occurs in medial position, but can also occur in sentence final position when functioning as a linking adverbial.

▶ *Though* can often separate a subject (noun phrase) from a verb (verb phrase).

While *so, then,* and *though* are often addressed in listening, speaking, and grammar texts, these features were identified from the *Longman Grammar of Spoken and Written English* and my (along with the help of a colleague) analysis of concordance lines for each signal word from taken from MICASE. See Figures 5.1 and 5.2 for concordances for *then* and *though* in MICASE.

TOOLS

Because this activity focuses on signal words specifically used in academic speaking and listening contexts, MICASE is the ideal corpus for this activity (we know its entire content is made of academic spoken English).

MICASE is a publicly available corpus that can be accessed online. At the time this book was published, MICASE contained 152 transcripts totaling 1,848,364 words. MICASE has an excellent built-in concordancer that allows users to search under specific parameters such as gender, education level, and context (e.g., a classroom setting, office hours).

Concordance lines for an activity of this type can be obtained by entering the node(s) into the MICASE concordancer, in this case *so, then,* and *though,* and reviewing approximately 500 lines for each node. Upon review of the 500 lines, salient features of the node, such as those previously mentioned, will become apparent. Lines to be used in the actual activity should be taken from the original 500 and chosen based on their difficulty level and straightforward display of the salient features or specific patterns.

Figure 5.1
Results of the Search Conducted for *then* to Design
the Corpus-Designed Activity on Signal Words

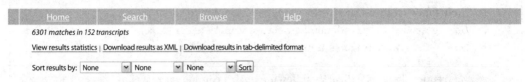

MICASE

| Home | Search | Browse | Help |

6301 matches in 152 transcripts

View results statistics | Download results as XML | Download results in tab-delimited format

Sort results by: None ▾ None ▾ None ▾ Sort

Transcript ID: (click to view)	Left Context	Match	Right Context	View context
LES280JG138	nt about getting people out at different ages, you'd have higher bonuses for younger people. mkay but	then	there's a question about should you be indifferent about getting rid of people at different ages? an	view
COL999MG053	young children so, a-as a rule i i try to get home, at a decent hour so we have meals, and uh, and	then	play with my kids, and um my wife and i make an honest attempt to get 'em to bed by nine o'clock, uh	view
LES405JG078	a, (bis toxins) to make sure they're flavored the right way. they made like, this, great tomato but	then	they used this but they used	view
SEM475JU84	y sort of um, connection with that body anymore. he remembers that his brain is back in Houston, and	then	he sort of i- reidentifies himself with the brain. he starts thinking okay, i must be that brain. an	view
OFC301MU021	mhm. um and	then	you can say, um well m- maybe not n- maybe not down to the last detail, um that_you n- maybe not i	view
MTG400MX008	re Heidi just put eighty-four nineteen on one line and drop twelve sixty-three down to the next line	then	put the results over to the right of there.	view
COL475MX082	solute power. but, before he's ordained anything, he can do it anyway. Sherlock.	then	notes the fears that go with the claim that God's power has no bounds and I quote. mankind, judge of	view

At the top of the page, you can view statistics about *then* or sort the results by what comes before or after *then*. In the far left column, you can view the entire transcript for each instance of *then*. In the far right column, you can view extended context (usually about 100 words) of the text immediately surrounding *then*.

Source: http://micase.elicorpora.info. Used with permission.

Figure 5.2
Concordance Lines for *though* Used to Design
the Corpus-Designed Activity on Signal Words

Transcript ID	Left Context	Match	Right Context	View
COL999MX040	of those four hundred PhDs thirteen have gone to women. i don't even want to think of the percent even	though	i'm, can do the math. um but i'm proud to say that four of these women were my students and um i've	view
TOU999MX062	t piece it doesn't necessarily have to be three-dimensional, but it's made for a specific site, and,	though	this artist, Gina Ferrari, um, has done thing, uh, similar to this they were not in this specific,	view
COL475MX082	John Clark of, Hull holds that God's will is the source of the obligation of the moral law	though	he allows that its content is not due purely to will. Chubb will have none of this insisting with Cl	view
SVC999MX148	yeah…it happens everyone once in a while. (haven't heard it lately	though	) what stops it?	view
SEM545MG083	mhm. right.	though	he does say that, that there is no, hostile undertone in, in the way they look at them.	view
LEL175JU086	o, that will make it more likely, that we get, away with it, that we enable our, plant to grow even	though	it's pusing, the envelope of the limits of hardiness of cold tolerance. now we can take a page, out	view
SEM475JU084	h. i think thr- the difference between three and five is kind of, difficult. i men, his i- his idea	though	is that, in um, where your point of view, three is, you are wherever you think you are. so, if you t	view
LAB205SU045	yes. okay, let me ask you a question. well before i ask you this question	though	, for this problem for this particular problem, in addition to what we just talked about that i woul	view
OFC285SG135	y that the way that the, the words being chosen the means of expressing these feelings, they feel as	though	they've been there many many many many times. an-	view
SGR175SU123	it, oh it di- it didn't	though	i would do it. but if it doesn't,	view
SGR999MX115	ah, but this isn't a pr- also	though	th- i don't think this is like detrimental t- lethal to objectivism this little, i mean this inconcsi	view
LAB175SU026	it sounds like something we're heard	though	i know that	view
LES315SU129	olutions, east of there in the s- Sudan, uh in Chad and Sudan, that um, were not, as closely related	though	the timing of them, uh could be said to be related, uh there was the Hausaland revolt of eighteen-oh	view
LEL220SU073	ow that a throne is also a chair, a stool is also a chair, a La-Z-Boy recliner is also a chair, even	though	these things don't have four legs, stool doesn't have a back, they can be made of metal not wood, bu	view

Source: http://micase.elicorpora.info. Used with permission.

PROCEDURES

After engaging students in a discussion about signal words, distribute copies of the *so* concordance lines (see Appendix 2B). As discussed in Chapter 4, it's important to walk the students through the first few lines in order to build their confidence about the straightforwardness of the activity, especially if this is their first time completing a corpus-designed activity. Ask students to analyze the concordance lines using the technique presented in Chapter 4, using a process similar to that presented here:

▶ Ask students to look at the first concordance line: *I wanna remind you that we do not have class on Thursday. This is to give you a chance to work on the midterm, so spend some time thinking about the midterm.*

▶ Direct students to highlight the word *so* in the first item: *I wanna remind you that we do not have class on Thursday. This is to give you a chance to work on the midterm, so spend some time thinking about the midterm.*

▶ Ask students to underline all of the words to the right of so until they reach the end of the sentence. For Number 1, they should underline *spend some time thinking about the midterm: I wanna remind you that we do not have class on Thursday. This is to give you a chance to work on the midterm, so spend some time thinking about the midterm.*

▶ Ask the students to highlight *so,* and underline all of the words in the sentence to the right of *so* in the rest of the items (as shown in Figure 5.3).

▶ Ask students what the underlined words in the sentences have in common. (They are independent clauses; in other words, if you deleted *so* from the examples in Figure 5.3, you would still have complete grammatical sentences and ideas.)

▶ Lead the students to draw the conclusion that *so* precedes an independent clause. Perhaps surprisingly, or perhaps not, students do notice the patterns that appear in the concordance lines and are able to draw conclusions about how the language features work. If, however, students appear at a loss, you can provide "hints" to help them deduce the featured patterns. If, for example, students do not seem to observe that *so* precedes an independent clause in the concordance lines, you can delete *so* from the lines and show students that complete grammatical sentences are left. This should help them draw the conclusion that *so* precedes an independent clause.

▶ Write this pattern on the board:

so + independent clause
so + complete sentence

▶ Now ask the students to look at the word immediately to the left of *so* in each sentence and to underline it. For Number 1, they should underline *midterm*. For Number 2, they should underline *and*.

Figure 5.3
***so* with All the Words to Right of *so* until the End of the Sentence Underlined**

1. so *spend some time thinking about the midterm.*
2. so, *the economic changes that have brought more and more women into the work force in the twentieth century have clashed with the inability of our society to deal with large numbers of women in the labor force.*
3. so *the reduction for the need for women's labor occurs among young, unmarried women in the home who formed some of the early factory workers in the early stages of industrialization in New England.*
4. so *it no longer is considered work.*
5. so *we see a real change by the 1870s and 80s in which women's colleges are drawing more young unmarried women into college educations.*
6. so *government propaganda was produced to get as many women into the work force as possible.*
7. so, *in your essays, every time you are referring to an article that you read, put it in parentheses.*
8. so *you have to move in accordance with the seasons.* When it's the dry season, you have to go to the few areas where there's a constant supply of water.
9. So, *because of the environment, they have to have that mobility, and that mobility is increasingly infringed upon by these different factors.*
10. So, *because of all these increasing pressures on them from outside forces, it has led to an increase of conflict from within.*
11. so *they don't have time to actually live life.*
12. so *you can raise your status in society by having given away and redistributed your belongings to everybody.*
13. so *sometimes virtually everybody that we'll be looking at historically, by the standards of today, would be considered a racist.*
14. so *you can understand the process.*
15. so *you just basically take all the traits and you weigh them all in various sorts of ways.*
16. so *you know he was always throwing up and he never could really sleep well.*
17. So, *let's look at his ideas.*
18. So, *once you decide that the reason that the sun rises in the east is because of the way the world is spinning, then you would predict the sun is gonna rise in the east again tomorrow.*
19. so *feel free to come down at any time.*
20. so *what I'm going to do is I'm going to label them.*

Figure 5.3 (cont'd)
***so* with the Word Immediately to the Left Underlined**

> **1** *I wanna remind you that we do not have class on Thursday. This is to give you a chance to work on the <u>midterm</u>, <u>so</u> <u>spend some time thinking about the midterm</u>.*
>
> **2** *Women who work hard and earn less bring less home to their families. <u>And</u> <u>so</u>, <u>the economic changes that have brought more and more women into the work force in the twentieth century have clashed with the inability of our society to deal with large numbers of women in the labor force.</u>*

▶ Ask students if they notice any patterns. (*And*, a comma, or a period frequently precede *so* as illustrated in Figure 5.4.) Students can also note that an independent clause also precedes *so*.

▶ Write the information students have discovered on the board.

▶ Ask the students to review and study both sentences in each line. Lead the students to draw the conclusion that *so* is used to tell how one point or idea moves to another point or idea, connecting the two clauses (or, your students may be more comfortable with the term *sentences* instead of *clauses*). As previously mentioned, students do tend to notice the patterns that appear in the concordance lines and are able to draw conclusions about how the language features work. If, however, students are having trouble, in this case articulating that *so* is used to tell how one point or idea moves to another point or idea, show the students the complete sentence with *so* deleted (e.g., Line 20 would read *Now the structures are too big to write here . . . what I'm going to do is I'm going to label them*) with a *1* written over the first half (*Now the structures are too big to write here...*) and a *2* written over the second half (*...what I'm going to do is I'm going to label them*). This should help them draw the conclusion that *so* is used to tell how one point or idea moves to another point or idea.

▶ Students may note that *so* does not always follow the patterns. This is an important point, as language in use is not always 100 percent anything and will sometimes not follow established patterns. Furthermore, students may notice additional patterns in the language that the teacher should encourage.

After studying the *so* concordance lines, pass out copies of the *then* concordance lines (see Appendix 2B).

▶ Ask students to look at the first line and highlight the word *then*: *1. You not only have a vacation today, but you have a vacation on Thursday, and* **then** *we'll be showing a movie on Tuesday.*

▶ Ask the students to underline the words that come after *then* but that are in the same sentence. For Number 1, they should underline *we'll be showing a movie on Tuesday*: *1. You not only have a vacation today, but you have a vacation on Thursday, and* **then** *<u>we'll be showing a movie on Tuesday</u>.*

Figure 5.4
and, a Comma, or a Period Frequently Precede so

1 *This is to give you a chance to work on the <u>midterm</u>, so*

2 *Women who work hard and earn less bring less home to their families. <u>And</u> so*

3 *Remember, surplus people are producing for surplus, <u>and</u> so*

4 *Gradually the notion of women's work sort of gets erased. It's not paid labor in the home, <u>and</u> so*

5 *Many of these young daughters began to continue to go through school till high school and then to college, <u>and</u> so*

6 *During World War Two, with large numbers of men leaving home, there was an extraordinary labor shortage, <u>and</u> so*

7 *I want it to be active <u>knowledge</u> so*

8 *I'm gonna show you some pictures of it, but this area of Kenya is very <u>arid,</u> so*

9 *During the rainy season, you have more opportunities to go elsewhere and take advantage of different grazing <u>areas. So</u>*

10 *All these communities which traditionally have been unregulated in their movements now are having to negotiate all these problems with ranches and government <u>policies. So</u>*

11 *People say they work all the time, <u>and</u> so*

12 *But in other societies, wealth is measured by many different <u>things,</u> so.*

13 *They come from a different place and a different <u>time,</u> so*

14 *You don't have to memorize this stuff; I'm offering this to you because it's a way of visualizing how it works, <u>and</u> so*

15 *You have so many traits that may not give you valid <u>information,</u> so*

16 *He was always <u>seasick</u> so*

17 *He really didn't do much except sit at home and work whenever he could and think about the collections that he'd <u>made. So</u>*

18 *Once we have the general principles, they allow us to make specific <u>predictions. So</u>*

19 *There's a lot of bagels <u>left,</u> so*

20 *Now the structures are too big to write <u>here,</u> so*

▶ Ask students to highlight *then,* and underline the words that come after it in every sentence. Be sure that students understand they are underlining the words that follow *then* in the same sentence, as shown in Figure 5.5.

▶ Ask what function the underlined words have in the sentences. (Many of the examples of the underlined words are verb phrases. Some of the underlined examples are independent clauses.)

▶ Lead the students to draw the conclusion that *then* is most often followed by a verb phrase, and sometimes followed by an independent clause. (See also page 61 for a strategy if students don't see the connections.)

Figure 5.5
then with the Words after It in the Same Sentence Underlined

1 _then_ _we'll be showing a movie on Tuesday._

2 _then_ _came the king,_ and _then_ _came the heads of the families, okay?_

3 _then_ _marry middle or upwardly mobile young farm men who were moving into the lower middle class._

4 _then_ _to college, and so we see a real change by the eighteen seventies a- and eighties in which women's colleges are founded and drawing more and more, young unmarried affluent women into college educations._

5 _then_ _eventually bolstered by the federal government._

6 _then_ _be able to explain to us how those two things are constantly interacting._

7 _Then, of course, that eats away again at traditional grazing areas that the Masai have always used. So that's yet another pressure._

8 _then_ _they are married women._

9 _then_ _redistributes it according to the needs of everyone in society._

10 _then_ _at the end of the harvest they'll give a certain portion of that over to the chief._

11 _then_ _goes on to talk about cultural ecology and says how other people started theorizing consumption in terms of, constraints given in the environment._

12 _then_ _have somebody's lawyer call me in the morning saying, my client was recorded against his will._

13 _then_ _things changed,_

14 _then_ _both of those ideas were out and a lot of more intelligent people thought that both worked._

15 _then_ _it'll give you a chance to review it because you can circle the stuff yourself._

16 _then_ _in the winter, the sun goes south for the winter._

17 _then_ _four American student leaders to talk about what international students might be doing to influence the departments through the student groups._

18 _then, ideally, after that you respond based on this information._

19 _then_ _deal with our rules and if you don't want to, then that's fine we've got many others that wanna take your place._

20 _then_ _slowly are changing through time, possibly the elevation hasn't changed enough uh during that period to influence the evolution of those plants as much._

▶ Write these patterns on the board:

1. _then_ + verb phrase
2. _then_ + independent clause

▶ Ask students to underline the word directly before _then_ in each of the lines. For Number 1, they should underline _and_. For Number 2, they should underline _and_. See Figure 5.6.

Figure 5.6
***then* with the Word Directly before It Underlined**

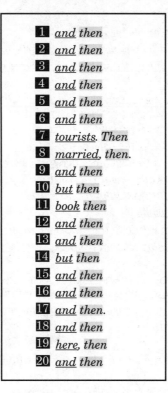

▶ Ask students if they notice any patterns, and lead them to draw the conclusion that *then* most often follows conjunctions (*and* and *but*). (See page 61 for strategies to help students.)

▶ Ask students to review and study the content of the sentences in each line; then, lead students to draw the conclusion that *then* is used to indicate addition, often to list items or events.

▶ Students may note that *then* does not always follow the patterns mentioned. Remember, this is an important point because language in use is not always 100 percent anything, and follows preferred, not absolute, patterns. Moreover, students may notice additional patterns, which should be encouraged. After studying the *then* concordance lines, pass out copies of the *though* concordance lines (see Appendix 2B).

▶ Ask students to look at the first line. Tell them at this point they should only concentrate on the second sentence in each line.

▶ Direct students to highlight the word *though* in the concordance lines as they've done with *so* and *then*: *1. The two disciplines do not appear on the surface to have very much in common. Historically, though, anthropologists and epidemiologists have worked together for a very long period of time.*

▶ Direct students to look at the punctuation immediately to the left and right of *though* in each line, as shown in Figure 5.7.

▶ Ask students what this punctuation might tell us. (*Though* is mostly set off by commas, which indicates it is in medial position. Some instances of *though* occur directly before a period, at the end of the sentence.) See Figure 5.7.

▶ After establishing that *though* most often occurs in medial position, ask students to underline the four words to the left of *though*. Then ask students what patterns they notice. (*Though* often follows either a noun phrase or a verb phrase.) See Figure 5.8.

▶ Write these patterns on the board:

1. NP + *though*
2. VP + *though*

▶ Ask students to review and study the content of the sentences in each line, and lead them to draw the conclusion that in both patterns *though* is used to show a contrast.

▶ Again, students may note that *though* does not always follow the mentioned patterns as language in use follows preferred, not absolute, patterns; this is an important point for students to understand. If students notice additional patterns, discuss them.

Once students discover and understand patterns and salient features related to the language feature at hand, a gap-fill exercise is appropriate. Remember, the methodology of *form, meaning, and use* is still important. The gap-fill for this specific activity is in Appendix 2B. The creation of a gap-fill exercise is also relatively simple: Using the original 500 concordance lines for each targeted feature, choose lines at an appropriate level and that have a straightforward display of the salient features or patterns (but the lines should be different from those used in the discovery exercise), delete the targeted feature from the lines, and then randomly mix them. Students can practice the meanings and patterns that they just learned by filling in the appropriate target features.

Don't forget to engage students in a whole language exercise. Applying what the students have discovered is as important as the discovery itself. Suggested whole language exercises for this activity are on page 119, Appendix 2B. Similar exercises are appropriate for any activity of this type.

Figure 5.7
Punctuation to the Immediate Left and Right of *though*

1. *The two disciplines do not appear on the surface to have very much in common. Historically, though, anthropologists and epidemiologists have worked together for a very long period of time.*

2. *Women are identified as being employed much less often than men. You can look at this as, we live in a world where producers are conceptualizing women as dependent on men. Remember, though, you can also look at it as: men's characters may be disproportionately shown as being employed.*

3. *We're gonna verify this answer, and then we're gonna discuss a little bit about why it is so surprising. To verify the answer, though, I need some help.*

4. *How many of you saw that movie? Don't see it, the rest of you who haven't; it's pretty bad. Unfortunately, though, I have to say that I worked on that film.*

5. *The book made a nice guide to the movie. It is confusing, though, which I must say I find really kind of amazing when you realize the simplicity of the language.*

6. *The Department of Engineering has awarded four hundred PhDs since 1958, though only thirteen of those have gone to women.*

7. *The item I'm trying to sort might actually already be in the right spot. Let's say it isn't, though, and small is different from start.*

8. *It's a fairly old paper, so if you want a copy of the paper you can go read it. It's not required that you get this paper, though.*

9. *If I put in the discount factor, though, um, it's going to differ not only between this segment and this segment, but it's going to get heavier and heavier the older I get.*

10. *Now a lot of people who don't speak like my uncle have a few words that people who know him well can understand. For the most part, he doesn't speak. He can be an excellent mime, though.*

11. *Meanwhile, I'm eager to hear what she has to say tonight, because Joan Jacobs Brumberg tells a stunning and troubling story. What is even more important, though, is that she not only tells us a fascinating and disturbing story, but she has some important ideas about how we might do better, in providing what adolescent girls need to survive.*

12. *Diary keeping has almost always been a middle class activity for a variety of reasons that have to do with affluence and styles of nurture. What's interesting, though, about the history of diaries is that they appear regularly among different ethnic minorities at that moment in the family history when the family has achieved middle class status.*

13. *Any other questions about the movie? What'd you think of it? I sorta liked it. There's so much covered in it though; it's real worth talking about it.*

14. *Well, in the first large cosmopolitan site, as long as the student's putting out good research, doing well in classes, the people really don't care how and (who) the support comes from. In the second site, though, it's a very much of a concern.*

15. *In the cosmopolitan huge site, somebody told me that no one needs any special attention. In the second site though, I found they were more concerned about the individual student here.*

16. *And so what's in that dark streak? There have been several claims as to what could be in that dark streak. We, though, did our own analysis, and uh found that it was F-E-three-O-four.*

17. *There's a technological view though, but the other view is to try and think of the environment the way the animal sees it and to try and think about an animal's eye view of the environment.*

18. *If you visit Williamsburg, you'll be struck because all of the buildings are reconstructed in Georgian style, and they do vary between brick and wood. The vast majority of the structures in Williamsburg, though, are made out of wood.*

19. *Well, it's possible. I wouldn't say that he's wrong though, necessarily.*

20. *In her recent work, she is clearly interested in the ordinary vicissitudes of adolescence for girls in contemporary America. She retains, though, a concern about the potential for the deeper trouble that some girls end up in.*

Figure 5.8
***though* with Four Words to the Left Underlined**

1. *much in common. Historically, though,*
2. *dependent on men. Remember, though,*
3. *To verify the answer, though,*
4. *it's pretty bad. Unfortunately, though,*
5. *movie. It is confusing, though,*
6. *four hundred PhDs since 1958, though*
7. *Let's say it isn't, though,*
8. *you get this paper, though.*
9. *in the discount factor, though,*
10. *be an excellent mime, though.*
11. *is even more important, though,*
12. *of nurture. What's interesting, though,*
13. *much covered in it though;*
14. *In the second site, though,*
15. *In the second site though*
16. *that dark streak. We, though,*
17. *There's a technological view though,*
18. *the structures in Williamsburg, though,*
19. *say that he's wrong though*
20. *contemporary America. She retains, though*

ON YOUR OWN

As discussed in Chapter 1, register is one of the main areas of language teaching addressed through corpus linguistics and corpus-designed activities. The activity presented in this chapter is a classic example of how this can be done. Students learned specifically about a linguistic feature particular to academic spoken English. Signal words are one of the most important aspects of academic listening and speaking, and by engaging in a corpus-designed activity like the one discussed, students can discover, understand, and apply salient features of the most common signal words in academic speech, helping them become better users of English and better academic students, as well as providing them with a newfound confidence in their knowledge of and ability in giving oral presentations.

1. Investigate the use of *so, then,* and *though* in MICUSP (http://micusp. elicorpora.info). What are some of the salient features learners should be aware of when using *so*, *then*, and *though* in academic writing? How do these differ from the features in MICASE discussed in this chapter.

2. Investigate the use of *so, then,* and *though* in the fiction subcorpus of the COCA (www.americancorpus.org). What are some of the salient features of *so, then*, and *though* that learners can expect to encounter in fiction? How do these features differ from those in academic speaking? From MICUSP?

Chapter 6

"That's so interesting!" Studying Vocabulary in an American Memoir

In the language classroom, there is no debate as to the importance of reading and the written word; in every English language program, one can find many classes dedicated to the instruction of reading, and every English language teaching publishing company offers a plethora of texts for teaching reading. In recent years, research has shown us that the teaching of extensive reading is also important for students, as it is useful for improving reading ability, linguistic competence, vocabulary, spelling, writing, and overall language proficiency (see Iwahori, 2008; Fredricks & Sobko, 2008; Day & Bamford, 1998; Green & Oxford, 1995; Nation, 1997). Although many programs encourage their students to read English books on their own to improve their language skills, some language programs are now also offering specific extensive reading classes to help students develop the aforementioned benefits associated with extensive reading; ELT publishers are also now offering more novels and extended texts in their product lines. Brown (2001) says that in teaching extensive reading, it can be tempting to simply assign students to read a certain number of pages with no introductions, hints, or follow-up activities; he suggests the use of the three-part framework—Before You Read, While You Read, and After You Read—to make the most of an extensive reading class. Many articles have offered activities for these frameworks to help instructors ensure students make the most of their extensive reading class (see Bamford & Day, 2004; Jacobs & Gallo, 2002; White 2007; Bennett, 2006).

As part of the 50th anniversary of the integration of Central High School in Little Rock, Arkansas, many first-year students at higher education institutions across the state were required to read *Warriors Don't Cry* (Washington Square Press, 1995), a novel written by Melba Pattillo Beals, one of the black teenagers chosen to integrate Central High following the passage of *Brown v. Board of Education of Topeka* (1954). The novel recalls her experiences and trials of that first school year at Central. This corpus-designed activity was created for high-intermediate to advanced English for Academic Purposes (EAP) students who were also required to read the novel and focuses on using extensive reading as a means for introducing academic vocabulary.

TARGET FEATURE: ACADEMIC VOCABULARY

The AWL (Coxhead, 2000) is a well-known example of using corpus linguistics to address ESP or EAP. Because the students reading *Warriors Don't Cry* were also enrolled in other credit-bearing academic courses, focusing on vocabulary from the Academic Word List seemed a productive way to combine their learning efforts. The vocabulary in the AWL is sorted according to frequency, with those words in Sublist 1 appearing most frequently. Sublist 1 was chosen as the starting point for vocabulary focus (see Table 6.1).

Words that appear on the AWL that were found in *Warriors Don't Cry* using Amazon Online Reader (see page 72) were selected for study in the EAP course. The list of selected words are shown in Table 6.2. In the interest of space, this activity only looks at the words *area, evident,* and *major*, but the process for all the words is identical.

Table 6.1
Most Frequent Member of the Word Families in Sublist 1 of the AWL

analyze	constitutional	evidence	indicate	occur	role
approach	create	export	individual	percent	section
area	data	factors	interpretation	period	sectors
assessment	definition	financial	involved	policy	significant
assume	derived	formula	issues	principle	similar
authority	distribution	function	labor	proceed	source
available	economic	identified	legal	process	specific
benefit	environment	income	legislation	required	structure
concept	established	context	major	research	theory
consistent	estimate	contract	method	response	variables

Source: www.victoria.ac.nz/lals/staff/averil-coxhead/awl/mostfreq1.html

Table 6.2
Words Used for Corpus-Designed Activities While Reading *Warriors Don't Cry*

response	issues	area	maintain	authority	focus
major	process	contract	involved	attitude	tradition
significant	evident	period	constant	circumstance	

TOOLS

Coxhead (2007, How to use this list) offers this advice for teaching the AWL:

1. Learners should read academic texts and listen to academic lectures and discussions. Where possible, the written and spoken texts should not be too difficult for learners, with no more than about 5 percent of the running words in the texts being new words for the learners.

2. Learners should have the chance to speak in academic discussion and write academic texts using academic vocabulary.

3. Learners should directly study words from the list using word cards and doing intensive study of short academic texts.

4. Learners should check the list for words they find in texts. If the words are in the AWL, they should learn them. If words are not in the list, students should check West's General Service List (1957). If the words are not in the most frequent 2,000 words of English or the AWL, then students should think carefully about whether or not the words need to be learned.

The concordance lines for the words in Table 6.2 were obtained using the Amazon Online Reader (AOR). AOR (www.amazon.com/exec/obidos/tg/browse/-/10197021) is a tool offered at Amazon.com for use with books in the Search Inside program. Essentially, AOR is a concordancing tool that uses the specific book as a corpus. Once a word or phrase is entered, the AOR displays the page number and an excerpt with the node highlighted. The page number also contains a link to view the actual page where the node is located—in other words, the extended context for some of the words. Figure 6.1 shows an example of an AOR display for the word *evidence* from *Warriors Don't Cry*. A typical AOR display shows the total number of occurrences of the word, the page number of each occurrence with a link to extended context, and a concordance line for each use of the word in the text.

In addition to the concordancing features of AOR, books in the Search Inside program also display a "concordance" feature. Amazon uses the term *concordance* a little bit differently than corpus linguists do, but for books in the Search Inside program, the *concordance* is an alphabetized list of the most frequently occurring words in the book, excluding function words such as *of* and other common words such as *it*. This is a handy tool. Figure 6.2 shows what the concordance for *Warriors Don't Cry* might look like. The font size of a word is proportional to the number of times it occurs in the book. Hovering a mouse over a word displays the total number of times the word is used in the book; *heard*, the smallest word in the concordance, is used 74 times in *Warriors Don't Cry*. *School*, the largest word in the display, is used 505 times in the book. Clicking on the word links to concordance lines for the word, as shown in Figure 6.1.[1] Other features of the Search Inside program include displaying the first sentence, key phrases, and the ability to browse the front and back covers and the first page.

---

1. The material in *Warriors Don't Cry* and other texts on Amazon.com is under copyright; ensuring that each student has his or her own copy of the text is important to honor copyright laws.

Figure 6.1
Examples of Results for the Node *evidence*

1. on Page 3:"
   "…I am at the same time very hopeful because I have ample **evidence** that what Grandmother promised me is true. With time and love, God solves all our problems. When we returned to…"
2. on Page 93:
   "…I had read in the newspaper that attorneys for the federal government would be arguing that there was no **evidence** of the kind of violence that made it necessary to call out troops. Since 93…"
3. on Page 101:
   "…means of National Guard troops. The judge's voice was deep, his tone emphatic, as he said, "There is no real **evidence** here that we shouldn't proceed with the court-ordered integration of Central High School…."
4. on Page 192:
   "…Melba Pattillo Beals cials had overwhelming **evidence** that our lives were in jeop- ardy, our information was nevertheless included. Yes, newspapers had printed the information before, but…"
5. on Page 231:
   "…He cited a recent order to that effect in Dallas, Texas, as **evidence** that Little Rock could do the same. …"

Figure 6.2
The 100 Most Frequently Used Words in *Warriors Don't Cry*

again always another arkansas asked away boy call called car central
class come day door down even eyes face faubus feel felt few first
friends front get girl go god going gonna good got governor
grandma group guard hand head heard help high home inside
integration keep knew know let life link little long looked mama man men
miinijean moment morning mother mrs myself new next nigger now
once people really right rock room say school see
segregationists soldiers something still stood students take talk tell things
think though thought time told two voice walked want wanted white
words year

PROCEDURES

The corpus-designed activity demonstrated here was used with students in each class of the academic session, focusing on a small number of words per class and corresponding to an assignment and discussion from *Warriors Don't Cry*. As an introduction to the course, students were informed about the AWL, given URL addresses for AWL activity sites (such as The Compleat Lexical Tutor www.lextutor.ca/ and Academic Vocabulary www.nottingham.ac.uk/~alzsh3/acvocab/), and introduced to the idea of corpus-designed activities.

Warriors Don't Cry was the first novel these EAP students had ever read or attempted to read in English. To build their confidence and orient them to the book, I used the Amazon concordance. First, I compiled the words from the Amazon concordance into a checklist format for students to review (see Appendix 2C). Students were given the list of words and asked to check the box for every word that they knew. *Integration* and *segregationists* proved a slight challenge to the students, as did the proper name *Faubus* (the governor of Arkansas during the Central High crisis). Otherwise, students were confident about the words on the list. Once students declared that they were confident with the list, I explained that these were the most frequent 100 words used in the book. Students were initially astounded, but then they were elated! With this one exercise, they gained enough confidence to believe they could read the entire novel. Next, we looked at the Amazon concordance on screen and explored the varying frequencies and some concordance lines for the words. At that time, students were given the list of words in Table 6.2. They were instructed to watch for these particular words as they were reading, both in *Warriors Don't Cry* and their other academic texts.

The corpus-designed activities used for these activities are similar to those discussed in Chapters 4 and 5 in that the students searched concordance lines for particular patterns. Students were instructed to look to the left and right of each word and notice any patterns. As previously mentioned, the words *major, evident,* and *area* will serve as examples for this corpus-designed activity in the interest of space. Figure 6.3 displays example concordance lines from *Warriors Don't Cry* for these words.

Studying these and other lines for *major*, students will note past tense verbs, determiners, and adjectives to the left of the node with negative nouns to the right for the pattern

(past tense) verb + determiner + (adjective) *major* + (adjective +) negative noun

Studying these and other lines for *evident*, students will notice the dummy subject *it* and past tense *was* to the left of the node and prepositions *in* and *from* as well as subordinators *as* and *that* to the right for the pattern

(*it+*) *was* + *evident* + preposition(/subordinator)

Figure 6.3
Example Concordance Lines for *major, evident,* **and** *area*

major

1 The one **major** change I could see was Mother Lois's attending still more classes at the white people's university.

2 The situation was fast becoming a **major** historical fight.

3 The day before Christmas the Gazette carried two **major** local stories.

evident

1 A hopeful mood was **evident** in the church service.

2 It was **evident** from that description that he wouldn't help us.

3 It was **evident** that school officials and teachers were under more and more pressure.

area

1 What had to stay in a separate **area**.

2 I pressed my thumb to the wounded **area** to try and stop the bleeding.

3 The cafeteria was one of the most dangerous **areas** of Central High's grounds.

Studying these and other lines for *area*, students will notice the preposition *in*, a determiner, and a negative adjective or adjective relating to size to the left of the node for the pattern

(*in* +) determiner + (adjective +) *area*

A follow up to the corpus-designed activity was a lecture on the vocabulary words compiled from information found in the *OCD* (2002) and other corpus-cited texts. Sample PowerPoint slides for these words can be found in Appendix 2C. After the lesson, students identified one or more of the targeted words in at least one authentic text (spoken or written) in their other courses for homework.

With electronic copies of a text, you can easily use the search function in either Microsoft Word or Adobe Acrobat to locate specific vocabulary words to then study their patterns. The Compleat Lexical Tutor also has various programs to analyze electronic texts for vocabulary words. Project Gutenburg is an Internet archive of approximately 30,000 copyright-free books stored as machine-readable text. Information about these sites can be found in Appendix 1.

ON YOUR OWN

This corpus-designed activity is different from the others in this book because it is more of a supplemental avenue to maximize learning that students are already engaged in. While corpus-influenced materials, corpus-cited texts, and corpus-designed activities maximize learning by nature, this corpus-designed activity worked in tandem with other class materials, integrating the corpus approach into an already established curriculum.

This corpus-designed activity is also different from the others discussed here because it highlights the academic vocabulary and the concept that they employ patterns, rather than specific instructional patterns. *Warriors Don't Cry* provided only 6–20 lines for each targeted vocabulary word, a less than desirable number, but not necessarily surprising given that the AWL words are specific to academic texts (not fiction or memoirs). Having been exposed to the patterns found in their reading text, actively looking for those words and patterns in their other texts, and following up the corpus-designed activity with corpus-cited information from the *OCD* (2002), students developed skills they can utilize beyond their first extensive reading experience.

1. Search for *area, evident,* and *major* in MICASE. Compare the collocations in the slides from Appendix 2C to search results for each word. How frequent is each collocation?

2. Look at the patterns for *area, evident,* and *major* in Appendix 2C. Investigate each word in MICUSP for the specified patterns. How common is each pattern? Are there other frequent patterns for the words?

Chapter 7

"I do that?"
Comma Errors in Students' Academic Writing

In making decisions about grammar in the L2 writing classroom, Byrd and Reid (1998) advocate beginning with learners rather than structures. Beginning with learners means needs analysis. Needs analysis involves multiple facets, one of which is error analysis, identifying learners' most frequent and salient errors. But engaging in error analysis doesn't mean trying to address all errors that a student makes. Ferris (2008) cautions against expecting error-free writing. Errors should be prioritized, and a select number chosen for instruction. Error analysis helps identify and prioritize language instruction. Computer-aided error analysis (CEA) is, quite simply, the use of computers to analyze learner errors in a learner corpus. Using CEA allows students to see from the beginning of a course what their specific trouble spots are and allows you as the instructor to pinpoint error feedback. See page 14 for a review of learner corpora.

The activity in this chapter focuses on CEA in an L2 writing course where the students were members of a matriculating freshman class. As mentioned in Chapter 6, many first-year students at higher education institutions in Arkansas were required to read *Warriors Don't Cry* (Pattillo Beals, 1995) as part of celebrations of the 50th anniversary of the integration of Central High School. The essays compiling the example learner corpus used in this chapter were written as a response to reading *Warriors Don't Cry*.

TARGET FEATURE: COMMA ERRORS

Specifically in L2 writing, four major categories can be explored using CEA: grammar, lexis, pragmatics, and discourse. The information and activities in this chapter center on grammar, but keep in mind that the tools and procedures can be replicated with a focus on lexis, pragmatics, or discourse.

TOOLS

Five tools are needed to engage in CEA with L2 writers. The tools are generally readily accessible.

1. **error tagging code (ETC).** The ETC serves as a framework for the error analysis, containing linguistic features for a grammar analysis.

2. **learner essays.** The assignments through which you want to investigate your students' writing compiled in a corpus.

3. **collaborators.** Colleagues, inside or outside your school or department who assist with tagging the essays to contribute to reliability/validity.

4. **concordancing program.** The computer program you use to access the corpus.

5. **classroom materials.** The materials developed as a result of analysis and presented to students.

Your grammar error tagging code (ETC) will be developed according the area of analysis you've chosen. The ETC in Table 7.1, which I developed with two colleagues[1] for use with the activity described in this chapter, contains 15 grammar-related errors. Many of the symbols and errors in the ETC no doubt look familiar to you: we relied on symbols commonly used to mark L2 writing.

The ETC in Table 7.1 contains very specific grammar errors because a more detailed analysis was desired. However, a more general approach is also an option. Ferris (2008) recommends using six general grammatical error categories when correcting writing:

1. verbs
2. noun endings
3. articles
4. word choice
5. sentence structure
6. mechanics

Many of the specific errors cited in Table 7.1 can easily fit into these general categories; a more general ETC is shown in Table 7.2. You might find it beneficial to begin with a general ETC, determine which larger area is most troublesome for your students, and then develop a specific ETC for that area.

---

1. Special thanks for Meredith Bricker and Anne Bruehler for their help with the ETC.

Table 7.1
Specific Error Tagging Code

Symbol	Error	Explanation
vt	verb tense	Incorrect verb tense
vf	verb form	Verb incorrectly formed
wo	word order	Incorrect or awkward word order
sva	subject-verb agreement	Subject and verb do not agree in number
art	article	Incorrect or missing article
sing/pl	singular/plural	Problem with the singular or plural of a noun
wf	word form	Incorrect word form
wc	word choice	Incorrect word choice
cs	comma splice	Comma inserted unnecessarily
frag	fragment	Incomplete sentence
ro	run-on	Two independent clauses joined with no punctuation
cap	capital	Capital letter needed
sp	spelling	Word incorrectly spelled
p	punctuation	Incorrect or missing punctuation
nonid	nonidiomatic	Not expressed this way in English
lc	lowercase	Use a lower case letter
--	join words	Put words together (class room)
#	space	Add a space or remove extra space
~	transpose	Transpose elements
pa	agreement	Pronoun/antecedent agreement
/	delete	Delete word
c	comma	Needs a comma inserted
o	word omitted	A word has been omitted from the sentence
po	possessive	Possessive error

Table 7.2
General Error Tagging Code

Symbol	Error	Explanation
v	verbs	Any error dealing with tense, subject-verb agreement, etc.
n	noun endings	Any error dealing with singular/plural endings, nominalization, etc.
a	article	Missing or incorrect articles
wc	word choice	Any error dealing with collocation, part of speech, etc.
ss	sentence structure	Any error dealing with word order, missing words, etc.
m	mechanics	Any error dealing with capitalization, spelling, etc.

PROCEDURES

Once you have an ETC that will address your teaching objectives and students, it's time to apply it. This involves learner essays and, ideally, the collaborator(s). Read through each essay, identify the errors, and tag them with the appropriate error tagging code. Generally an underscore _ and the code are added to the offending word; they become part of the word to make the tag. This makes it easier to search for codes later. Figure 7.1 shows what part of a tagged essay looks like with the tags shaded. The essay in Figure 7.1 took approximately 20 minutes to read and tag. The collection of tagged essays is your learner corpus. See page 14 for more on tagging.

Asking a colleague to also tag the essays can increase reliability since you'll have more than one eye catching the errors and more than one voice determining error types. While some errors are obvious and more objective (e.g., subject-verb agreement), others can be more subjective (e.g., comma usage), so a discussion of what types of errors to mark is necessary.

At this point intellectual property must be addressed. All written work belongs to its author, even a writing assignment from an ESL/EFL class. Therefore, it's imperative to obtain written consent for use of that work, even for an in-class project such as the one described here. For a larger-scale project, you may even need permission from your school's IRB. (An example consent form for this activity is found in Appendix 2D.)

The fourth tool in this activity is a concordancing program. A concordancing program allows access to a corpus—in this case, the learner corpus of tagged essays. The figures and activities in this chapter were designed using TextSTAT; other concordancing programs that could be used in this activity are given in Appendix 1. See pages 16–18 for a review of concordancing programs.

Figure 7.1
A Tagged Learner Essay

Melba was a warrior in warriors_*cap* don't_*cap* cry_*cap*. She always planned where to be for not being attacked, she was not disappointed as warriors_*?*, she reacted with non_*#* violence, and she had suffered not only for her benefit but also for the right_*pl* of the black people who was_*sva* not allowed to attend whites' school.

First, while Melba was with_*o* other eight_*~* Little Rock_*c* their conversation had became_*nonld* to advise one another where to be for_*wc* not being_*wc* attacked, the reason why they no longer went in_*wc* places where they could be attacked easily_*c* like:_*/* in the cafeteria_*ro* for example_*c* melba had decided to bring her sandwich and eat being_*/* in a safe place, in other places like in the restroom, the corridors,_*o* ... where they could not escape easily_*?*, this show_*sva* that she_*/* that_*/* Melba had became_*vf* a warrior who had to decide where to be,_*cs* to protect her self.

Second, Melba didn't_*/* be_*vt* disappointed in her life at Central High when white students was_*sva* kicking her, spiting_*sp* in her face_*c* and insulting her in_*wc* impolite words,_*ro* this show_*sva* that Melba was a warrior because it is not every one who can have this courage of not being disappointed except a warrior.

Even though white students do_*vt* bad thing_*pl* upon_*wc* Melba, she reacted with no violence_*c* and this is a_*art* unbelievable thing that I find Melba has done_*ro* which make_*sva* her a warrior,_*cs* because it not easy for a human who suffer_*sva* and not become angry and react violently, and for me she is beyond my belief to be a warrior like there_*nonid*.

However, Melba had_*vt* suffered not only for her benefit_*c* but also for the right_*pl* of the black people who was_*sva* not allowed to attend whites' school_*c* and art_*art*_person_*o* who scarifies_*sp* her life for others so that they can improve their way of being for me is_*~* a great warrior,_*cs* because she knew that she can_*vt* even die during the torture at central_*cap* high_*cap*_*c* but she didn't give up as a warrior on the battle field.

Therefore, according to my view in the given examples above_*/* of Melba's life at central_*cap* high_*cap* from the book warriors_*cap* don't_*cap* cry_*cap*, I conclude that Melba was a warrior in warriors_*cap* don't_*cap* cry_*cap*.

Use the concordancing program to determine the frequency of each error tag. Figure 7.2 shows how TextSTAT identified and displayed 14 _*wc* tagged errors in the learner corpus. A step-by-step guide to using TextSTAT for this type of activity is on pages 87–92. Use each tag from the ETC, _*wc* for example, as the node enables the concordancing program to identify the frequency of errors in the corpus, and then to display each of the errors. Table 7.3 shows the frequency of each error in the learner corpus. Because comma errors comprised more than 20 percent of the total number of errors, comma usage was singled out as the topic of the corpus-designed activity.

In order to better understand the types of comma errors the students had made, all the lines that contained comma errors were studied; from these lines, six types of comma errors were identified. Due to its high error frequency (see Figure 7.3), comma use with coordinating conjunctions was chosen as one type of error to pinpoint. Comma use with subordinators and academic language was also chosen due

Figure 7.2
_wc Errors in the Learner Corpus

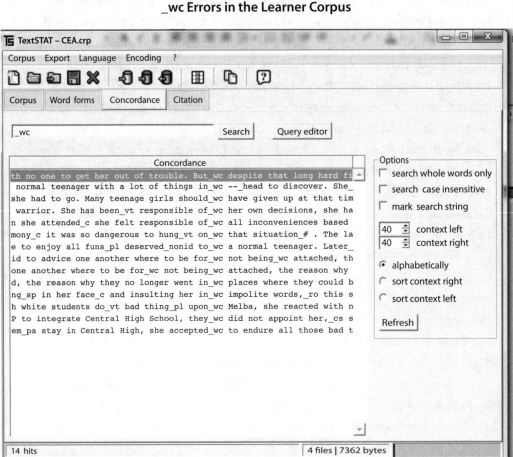

Table 7.3
Frequency of Errors in the Learner Corpus

Error	Raw #	% of Total Errors
vt	17	10
vf	3	2
wo	0	0
sva	7	4
art	2	1
sing	2	1
pl	15	9
wf	3	2
wc	15	9
cs	**5**	**3**
ro	3	2
cap	23	14
sp	2	1
p	2	1
nonid	4	2
#	6	4
~	3	2
pa	3	2
/	10	5
c	**34**	**20**
o	10	5
po	1	1
- -	0	0
frag	0	0
lc	0	0
Total	170	100

Bold indicates an error involving commas.

Figure 7.3
Comma Errors in the Learner Corpus

sva not allowed to attend whites' school_c and art_person_pl who scarifies_wf her_—**CC**

was determined to fight for integration_c and determination is one of_o character—**CC**

almost all her hobbies for her new life_c and o_was not supported by her circle b—**CC**

n_wc Melba, she reacted with no violence_c and this is a_art unbelievable thing th—**CC**

had_vt suffered not only for her benefit_c but also for the right_pl of the black—**CC**

_pl do their evil thing without reacting_c but as she knew that not responding to—**CC**

fought for_? was attending a good school_c but it also meant a lot for black peopl—**CC**

in Central High_c refused to participate_c but Melba kept going forward even if sh—**CC**

rls should_wc have given up at that time_c but Melba was more perseverant than eve—**CC**

ring the torture at central_cap high_cap_c but she didn't give up as a warrior on—**CC**

rrior is not only someone going to fight_c but someone who fights till the end wit—**CC**

went through a wild life at Central High_c like having her peers chasing her, spit—**S**

aces where they could be attacked easily_c like:_/ in the cafeteria_ro for example—**S**

like:_/ in the cafeteria_ro for example_c melba had decided to bring her sandwich—**AL**

s it is only done by real warriors. Thus_c Melba was a real warrior. —**AL**

wing eggs or flying burnt objects on her_c or even hearing those bad quotes everyd—**L**

opposing their presence in Central High_c refused to participate_c but Melba kept—**S**

Once more_c the fact that some students_c seeing that there was_pl people opposin—**S**

participate_o, once inside Central High_c she accepted to not fight back as that—**S**

ved_nonid to_wc a normal teenager. Later_c she has been_vt surprised by how everyb—**AL**

inside the school, and when she attended_c she felt responsible of_wc all inconven—**S**

g, and even though her life was changing_c she had one general goal to reach. Firs—**S**

ious problems. Second, as a young person_c she really did not like to stand there—**S**

serious dangerous segregationist actions_c such as to be_vf kicked_# , to be_vf in—**AL**

haracteristic_pl of a warrior. Once more_c the fact that some students_c seeing th—**S**

e endured was too much for a little girl_c the result is_vt worth it. Not only int—**S**

lba was with_o other eight_~ Little Rock_c their conversation had became_wc to adv—**S**

p Melba_c as one of the Little Rock Nine_c was a warrior. She accepted_wc to parti—**A**

ow_cap Melba was_cap a warrior_cap Melba_c as one of the Little Rock Nine_c was a—**A**

_sva kicking her, spiting_sp in her face_c and insulting her in_wc impolite words,—**L**

e whole year. According to her testimony_c it was so dangerous to hung_vt on_wc th—**PP**

Coordinating conjunction=CC
Listing=L
Appositive=A
Prepositional phrase=PP
Subordinator=S
Academic language/transition phrase=AL

to its usefulness to L2 writers. Comma errors were chosen for this group of learners, but you may find that the most frequently made errors are not necessarily the most salient errors to your students.

Once the targeted error has been identified, it's time to make classroom materials! Three types of materials work best with CEA (regardless if your CEA involves a specific grammar ETC or a general discourse ETC):

1. consciousness raising/noticing activities
2. traditional grammar activities
3. authentic language activities

Consciousness raising/noticing activities involve students working with the actual concordance lines that contain the errors; that's all the lines that have comma errors. Figure 7.4 shows the lines from the concordance that contain a comma error with a subordinator; they have been "cleaned up" for student use in an activity. (All the lines with comma errors can be found in Appendix 2D to be used as an actual activity.) Ask students to look at each sentence. If necessary, guide them to determining the error in the sentence. This consciousness raising/noticing activity shows students their errors in context and draws their attention to the error.

Figure 7.4
Lines Containing a Comma Error with Subordinators

Melba went through a wild life at Central High like having her peers chasing her.

Their conversation became about things like places where they could be attacked easily like in the cafeteria.

Seeing that there were people opposing their presence in Central High some students refused to participate.

The fact that some students seeing that there were people opposing their presence in Central High....

Once inside Central High Melba accepted to not fight back.

When she attended Central High Mebla felt responsible for the inconveniences.

Even though her life was changing she had one general goal to reach.

Second, as a young person she really did not like to stand there.

Even though what she endured was too much for a little girl the result was worth it.

When Melba was with the other Little Rock Nine their conversation became different.

A consciousness raising/noticing activity can be followed by a traditional grammar activity. If the problem is with verb tense, find a section on verb tenses in a grammar book, present the grammar, and give practice exercises. To help students understand comma usage with coordinating conjunctions, subordinators, and academic language, materials on sentence type and transition words were created and are found in Appendix 2D.

Students need an authentic language exercise where they proofread an essay to find comma errors. In other words, the authentic language activity imitates the actual activity, giving students authentic proofreading/editing practice and encouraging autonomy. The essay students proofread for this activity can be found in Appendix 2D. This essay replicates the language used and errors made by the students. Ultimately, the students proofread their own essays for comma usage before turning them in for a final grade.

A traditional assessment of students' use of the target features before and after an activity is an effective way to document progress. Using the latest examples of student writing, assessments after the task could occur both immediately after students turn in a final draft as well as at the end of the course.

ON YOUR OWN

While it is of course possible to use error analysis without the aid of a concordancing program, completing a CEA can help you to make more informed choices about targeting errors. Seeing the errors in context allows you to determine exactly why the error is being made and can also help you prioritize salient errors.

To help our students become better writers, we must address grammatical errors, and for there to be progress, targeted instruction is necessary. One of the best ways to target errors in L2 writing today is through the use of a computer. Granger (1998, p. 6) points out that "learner corpora give us access not only to errors but to learners' total interlanguage." Instructors may be aware of their students' difficulties, but error analysis through a computer is the most feasible way to uncover error in context and become more aware of general performance. CEA discloses pedagogical need and can also lead to increased autonomy, an essential skill for error improvement in L2 writing. In sum, CEA is a tool you can use to put your learners first, target instruction, and facilitate writing proficiency.

1. Review and follow the step-by-step guide for using TextSTAT on pages 87–92 to complete your own CEA.

A Step-by-Step Guide to Using TextSTAT in a CEA Activity

Step 1. Open TextSTAT and select the "New Corpus" button, first from the left.

Figure 7.5
Create a New Corpus

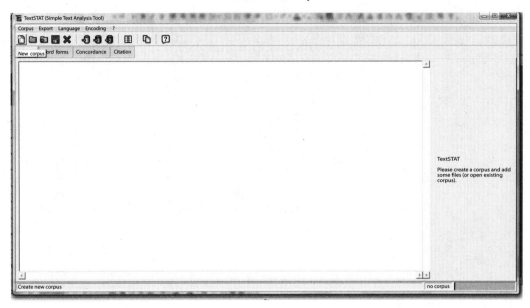

Step 2. Title your corpus. Here, I've titled the corpus "Computer Aided Error Analysis."

Figure 7.6
Name the Corpus

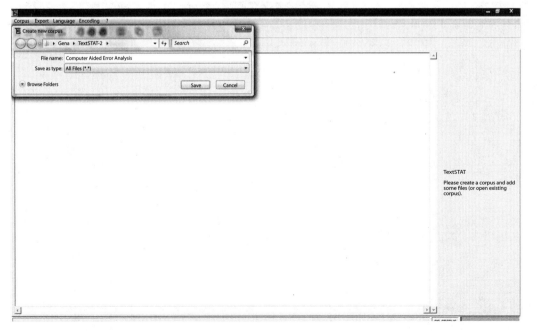

Step 3. When the encoding message pops up, select the OK button.

Figure 7.7
Click OK

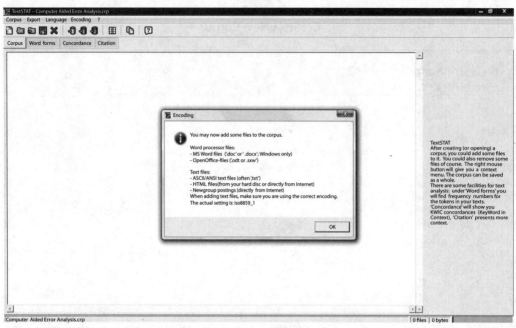

Step 4. Choose the "Add local file" button, seventh from the left.

Figure 7.8
Add Local File

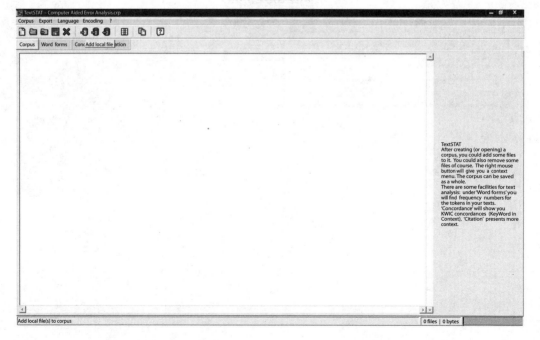

Step 5. Select a student's essay from your file directory. Files can be in .doc or .txt format.

Figure 7.9
Select Text

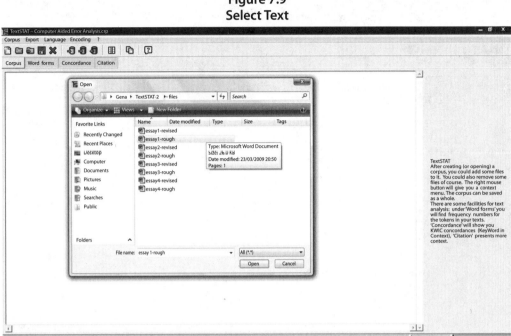

Step 6. Repeat Steps 4 and 5 until all the essays have been selected and added to your "corpus." (Alternatively, you can select all the essays at one time by holding down the Shift key.)

Figure 7.10
Add Text

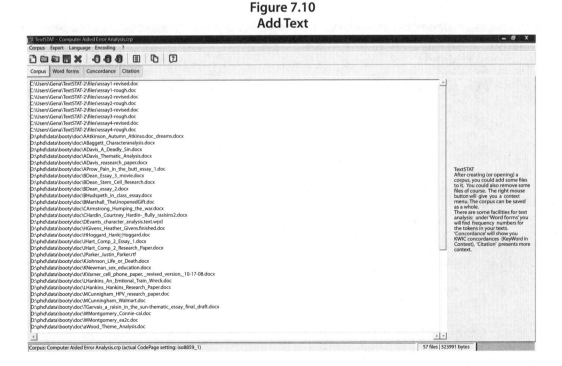

Step 7. Select the Concordance button, third tab from the left.

Figure 7.11
Create a Word List

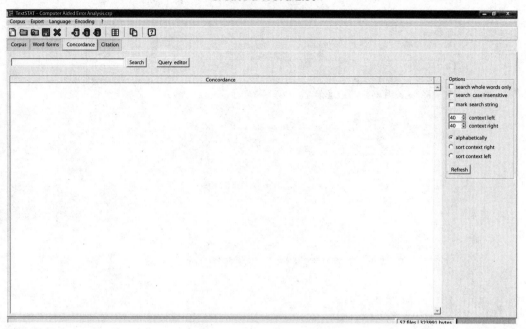

Step 8. Enter error tag into the box, and press the Search button.

Figure 7.12
Enter Node

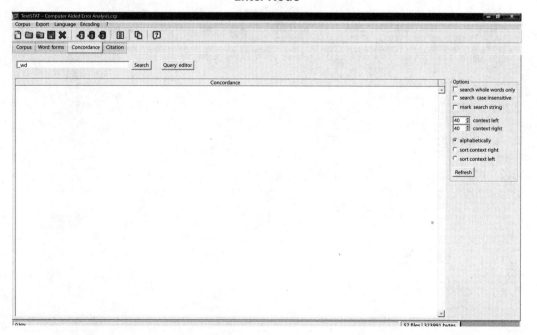

Step 9. All the lines containing that particular error tag will then appear. (You can only view one error at a time.) To view other error types, simply type another error tag into the search box.

Figure 7.13
View Concordance Lines

Step 10. Double click on any line to see extended context for that line with the error highlighted.

Figure 7.14
View Extended Context

Step 11. To save the lines (for studying, as shown in Figure 7.3), click the Export button, and choose your preferred file type. (Choosing MS Word usually makes the lines easier to manipulate.)

Figure 7.15
Export Concordance Lines

Step 12. A new window will open with the lines exported into a document. Be sure to save the document to your hard drive.

Figure 7.16
View Concordance Lines in MS Word

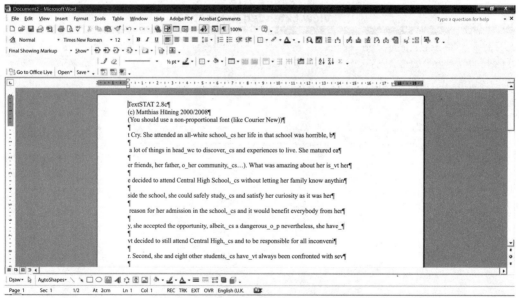

Step 13. The lines can now be manipulated in any fashion (highlighted to denote a category, cleaned up for students' use, etc.).

Chapter 8

Final Thoughts on Using Corpora in the Classroom

A list and discussion of the main ideas conveyed throughout the text follow. In addition, Table 8.1 offers a holistic view of using corpora in the classroom. Since the chapters are organized around particular language features and Appendix 1 contains a table organized by corpus tools and resources, Table 8.1 focuses on language skill and provides a complete view of using corpora in the classroom.

■ *This is not a theory book on corpus linguistics.* The main purpose of this book is to provide a general orientation to the routines involved in accessing and evaluating information from a corpus in order to present effective applications of corpora to classroom teaching. This book is intentionally light on the theoretical side. That being said, I have tried to provide an understanding of what the corpus approach entails so that you may transfer what you've learned here to your own classroom.

■ *Using corpora can provide a unique element of learning to your classroom.* Teaching with corpora is, obviously, not a "end all be all" to language teaching, but using corpora in the classroom can certainly facilitate language acquisition. More effective classroom materials engage learners in actual language use and in a variety of registers, which ultimately leads to increased motivation and more targeted learning. Used in conjuction with other materials (textbooks) and teaching approaches, corpora provide learners with the tools needed for language acquisition.

■ *All language skills can be taught using corpora.* The activities demonstrated establish the broad range of application of teaching with corpora: from vocabulary to academic speaking, and using corpus-influenced materials to corpus-designed activities. Even the core principles of corpus-cited references and corpus-designed activities presented in each chapter can be applied to other language skills. For example, Chapter 5 discusses a corpus-designed activity that will help students in academic speaking. But the same technique can be used with a writing corpus to help students with academic writing.

■ *Don't feel intimidated or overwhelmed at the thought of working with corpora.* Many instructors feel intimidated at the thought of working with corpora. Using the corpus approach in your classroom can be time consuming, especially at first, and does require some training, like that provided in this book. However, once you're familiar with the methods and available tools and get some practice, using corpora in the classroom can become second nature.

■ *Corpora is not a "buzzword."* Some instructors are not interested in using corpora because they think it's a "buzzword" in language methodology, something trendy that will eventually fade. This book has demonstrated the merits of teaching with corpora and provided a clear rationale and justification, as well as demonstrated benefit, for using corpora in the classroom.

■ *Corpora don't have to be for "special" courses or class periods.* Ideally, a corpus-designed activity would be used with every lesson in every language course. While that may not be possible in all circumstances, corpus-influenced materials or corpus-cited texts can always be used. In fact, corpus-influenced materials, corpus-cited texts, and corpus-designed activities can all be used together, but the use of even just one of the corpus materials can maximize learning in your classroom.

■ *Corpus linguistics is for teachers.* Perhaps the most important goal of this text is to show that corpora are for teachers. They can help teachers; they are not just for linguists and researchers. The corpus approach is applicable and useful to classroom teachers and language learners everywhere.

Table 8.1
Corpora across the Curriculum

Skill	Reading	Writing	Speaking/ Listening/ Pronunciation	Grammar	Vocabulary
Textbooks	College Reading	Teaching a Lexis-Based Academic Writing Course	Academic Listening Strategies	Grammar In Use	Building Academic Vocabulary
		Touchstone			
	Four Point Reading and Writing		College Oral Communication	Natural Grammar	Vocabulary in Use
	Thinking Beyond the Content	Cambridge Grammar of English			In the Know
		Longman Grammar of Spoken and Written English			Teaching a Lexis-Based Academic Writing Course
		Oxford Collocations Dictionary			
		Academic Writing for Graduate Students	Academic Interactions		Focus on Vocabulary
		College Writing	Academic Listening Strategies		College Vocabulary
			Four Point Listening and Speaking		Focus on Vocabulary
					Vocabulary Power
					Vocabulary Mastery
Language Focus	AWL	Discourse Markers	Signal Words	Articles	AWL
	Cohesion	Error Correction			Collocations
		Lexical Bundles			
	Mental Verbs	Noun phrases	Reformulations	Stance	Phraseology
	Criticality	Pre/Post Modifiers	Backchannels	Verb Functions	
	Collocations	Introductory *it* and *that* clauses	Attention Signals	*that* Clauses	
		Linking Adverbials	Question Tags	Adverbials	
		Referring Expressions	Polite forms	Lexico-grammar	
		Existential *there*	Reduced Forms	Register	
		Tense	Fillers/Inserts	Tense	
		Assertions	Collocations		

Table 8.1 (continued)
Corpora across the Curriculum

Skill	Reading	Writing	Speaking/ Listening/ Pronunciation	Grammar	Vocabulary
Tools	MICUSP	CorpusLab	MICASE	CorpusLab	MICASE
	TextSTAT				
	COCA				
	WordSmith Tools				
	Amazon Reader	MICUSP	The Compleat Lexical Tutor	Sketch Engine	Amazon Reader
	The Compleat Lexical Tutor			The Compleat Lexical Tutor	SketchEngine
				CANDLE	The Compleat Lexical Tutor
				MICUSP	MICUSP
				MICASE	

Appendix 1

Corpora and Concordancing Tools

This is a list of corpora, concordancing programs, and other corpus tools readers may find useful. While this list is by no means exhaustive, the tools listed here are included specifically for their accessibility and ease for completing the types of activities discussed in this text.

Name	Description	On the Web	Availability
BNC Sampler	The BNC (British National Corpus) is a 100 million–word collection of samples of written and spoken language from a wide range of sources, designed to represent a wide cross-section of current British English, both spoken and written. The BNC Sampler allows users to see up to 50 random lines from the corpus for any search word or phrase.	www.natcorp. ox.ac.uk/	Free
CANDLE	With CANDLE (Corpora and Natural Language Processing for the Digital Learning of English), users can search for common collocations and patterns of nouns, verbs, and adjectives found in five different corpora. CANDLE was originally developed specifically for university-level Taiwanese students, but can be useful to any English language students.	http://candle. cs.nthu.edu. tw/collocation/ webform2. aspx?funcID=9	Free
Collins Cobuild Concordance and Collocation Sampler	The Sampler is a free concordancing and collocations sampler from the The Collins Cobuild Wordbanks*Online* corpus (which contains approximately 56 million words of contemporary written and spoken English) that displays the top 100 collocations of a word or phrase as well as 40 concordance lines for a word or phrase.	www.collins. co.uk/corpus/ CorpusSearch. aspx	Free
The Compleat Lexical Tutor	The Compleat Lexical Tutor contains a plethora of activities and tools for data-driven learning focusing on academic vocabulary. Tools include a concordancer, vocabulary profiler, exercise maker, diagnostic tests, and interactive exercises.	www.lextutor.ca/	Free
Corpora List	Links to word lists, web concordancers, bibliographies, and a corpora e-list.	http://nora. hd.uib.no/ corpora/	Free

Name	Description	On the Web	Availability
CorpusLab	CorpusLab is designed to promote language learning based on real English used in different settings. Teachers can create exercises—including gap-fill, multiple choice, matching, reorder, and categorize it—that are designed to promote learning of collocations and phrasal patterns. The site is also designed for the sharing of corpus resources and corpus-informed materials such as word lists, handouts, PowerPoints, etc. In addition, teachers have access to a corpus of spoken professional English via a simple concordancer. A utility for the analysis of potential teaching texts is also under development. CorpusLab has a grammar component and a writing component.	www.corpuslab.com/	Free with registration
Davies / BYU	Corpora that have been created by Mark Davies, Professor of Corpus Linguistics at Brigham Young University, including the COCA.	www.americancorpus.org	Free
Devoted to Corpora	A major compilation of existing corpora, along with descriptions and, where applicable, access information.	http://personal.cityu.edu.hk/~davidlee/devotedtocorpora/corpora.htm	Free
GlossaNet	GlossaNet allows users to generate concordances from daily editions of more than 100 newspapers that cover twelve European languages.	http://glossa.fltr.ucl.ac.be/	Free
ICE	ICE, the International Corpus of English, is a collection of corpora of various national and regional varieties of English. Each ICE corpus consists of one million words of spoken and written English.	www.ucl.ac.uk/english-usage/ice/avail.htm	Varies
Just the Word	JustTheWord displays the most common clusters (or phrases) for any search word along with extended context in which each cluster appears.	http://193.133.140.102/JustTheWord/index.html	Free
LDC	The Linguistic Data Consortium supports language-related education, research, and technology development by creating and sharing linguistic resources: data, tools, and standards. You can search the LDC catalog for existing available corpora.	www.ldc.upenn.edu/	Varies
LessonWriter	LessonWriter automatically creates lesson plans and instructional materials for teaching English language skills—by analyzing text vocabulary, grammar and usage, pronunciation, and word roots and stems—in the context texts that users can upload to the site.	www.lessonwriter.com	Free with registration

Name	Description	On the Web	Availability
MICASE	The MICASE (Michigan Corpus of Academic Spoken English) contains more than 1.8 million words of spoken language exclusively representing speech from university settings, including advising sessions, labs, office hours, colloquia, seminars, study groups, small and large lectures, and student presentations. Select audio files and transcripts are freely available on the website (with others available for purchase). *The MICASE Handbook* (Simpson-Vlach & Leicher, 2006) contains abstracts of all 152 speech events included in the corpus; speech events organized by type of speech event, academic division, interactivity rating, participant level, and characteristics of the primary speaker; and guidelines for developing pedagogical materials and sample MICASE-based instructional materials, is also available for purchase at www.press.umich.edu/esl/.	http://micase.elicorpora.info	Free access with additional resources available for purchase
MICUSP	The Michigan Corpus of Upper-level Student Papers contains more than 800 academic writing from upper-undergraduates and graduate students representing at least 16 disciplines from humanities and arts, social sciences, biological and health sciences, and physical sciences.	http://micusp/elicorpora.info	Free
MonoConc Pro	MonoConc Pro is a concordance program that provides KWIC concordance results, word lists, and collocation information. The program also comes with a range of features such as Context Search, Regular Expression search, Part-of-Speech Tag Search, Collocations, and Corpus Comparison.	www.athel.com/mono.html	$85 for individual license
OANC	The OANC (Open American National Corpus) contains more than 15 million words from the Second Release of the larger American National Corpus.	www.americannationalcorpus.org/OANC/index.html	Free
PIE	Using a subcorpus of the BNC, PIE (Phrases in English) is an independent concordancer that allows for the study of the distribution of words and phrases up to eight words long, including common phrases, phrase frames, grammatical patterns, and suffixes, prefixes, and words.	http://pie.usna.edu/	Free
Project Gutenberg	An Internet archive of approximately 30,000 copyright-free books stored as machine-readable text.	www.gutenberg.org/wiki/Main Page	Free

Name	Description	On the Web	Availability
Sketch Engine	Sketch Engine offers tools to understand how words behave, including word sketches (a one-page, automatic, corpus-derived summary of a word's grammatical and collocational behaviour), grammatical relations, and a distributional thesaurus. The site also contains pre-loaded corpora (60M-2B words) for Chinese, English, French, German, Italian, Japanese, Portuguese, Spanish, and Slovene; tools to build your own corpus to extract keywords and investigate specialist terminology in any language; and a CorpusBuilder to upload and install your own corpora.	www.sketchengine.co.uk/	Free 30-day trial; an individual license is €50 ($80)
TextSTAT	TextSTAT, Simple Text Analysis Tool, is a basic concordancer that allows users to upload files for corpus creation, access word lists for retrieving word forms, view concordance lines, and access extended context.	http://neon.niederlandistik.fu-berlin.de/textstat/	Free
WebCorp	WebCorp is a suite of tools that allows access to the World Wide Web as a corpus. WebCorp is particularly useful to study words and phrases that are too new or too rare to appear in a standard corpus.	www.webcorp.org.uk/guide/	Free
WordSmith Tools	WordSmith Tools is a comprehensive concordancer with three main tools: key words (words that occur unusually frequently in a corpus in comparison with a reference corpus); word list (a list showing how often each word occurs in the text files, what that is as a percent of the running words in the text, and how many text files each word was found in); and concordancing (a concordance of all the occurrences of a node in the text files of the corpus, including number of entries, where the entry occurs, and in what file it occurs).	www.lexically.net/wordsmith/	50 GBP ($80) individual license

Class Materials

ARTICLES

CONCORDANCE LINES FOR *a*

You need to take a hard look at it.

Lynn thinks she has a puzzling personality.

Ten years ago, he confessed to a brutal double murder.

It's like you're a different person.

A convicted killer proclaims he's innocent.

At least we think it's a good idea.

He entered her apartment in North Stockton, armed with a handgun.

We finally have added a fuel surcharge.

He's opened a restaurant, had his own cologne, and even starred in a music video.

Can you make it up in a spray-on can?

I must acknowledge a certain disappointment because I had hoped for more in my discussions with the Foreign Minister.

There's genuine anxiety about a prolonged deployment in an inhospitable region.

Some say their military will not accept a sensible foreign policy.

It's making a big splash now, but some industry analysts are wondering what will happen next.

Those who are not willing to work will have a hard time.

Why does our society permit so many of its children to have such ready access to a product that does so much harm?

A ship loaded with Indian refugees from Kuwait arrived in Dubai today.

I would take a whole box.

Let's talk a little bit about the savings and loan crisis.

Poindexter and MacFarland decided it was a better idea to lie to Congress.

Source: Corpus of Contemporary American English

CONCORDANCE LINES FOR *the*

You were talking about the President fearing the reaction of markets to such a speech.

When Hitler's war ended, there were the Nuremberg trials.

Well, the Air Force intelligence has it, obviously.

We're at the Taj Mahal in Atlantic City.

People are suggesting a cutback in the rate of growth of Medicare.

It wouldn't happen at the IRS.

Things keep going wrong on the space shuttle Columbia.

To make things even better, the Soviets have agreed to build at least ten commercial ships for Pepsi.

The fact is that this is a very bad time for Americans can't be ignored.

Before you ask whether there is a double standard in the U.N. resolution, there has to be some reference to its content.

We have terrified the Europeans, who think we are going to start a war immediately.

David asks about sensitive documents that might embarrass the United States generally or the current administration in particular.

The Sierra Club has split ranks with Earth.

The City of Norwalk contributes $3 million a year to the operating budget.

Thousands of Americans in the Persian Gulf are doing the same.

At first, they said war in the Middle East was inevitable.

U.S. intervention seems highly unlikely. Steve Shepard, ABC, the State Department.

At St. Matthew's Cathedral, Kerry Kennedy, daughter of the late Robert F. Kennedy, married Andrew Cuomo.

Silver Ending is the fastest finishing horse in the Derby field.

One criminologist suggested there was a chilling similarity to the Bundy cases.

Source: Corpus of Contemporary American English

———————— **Gap-Fill Activity** ————————

Fill in the blank with the *or* a.

1. _____ AAA survey which just come out today shows the falling price of gasoline.

2. The Free Democrats have _____ more radical, youthful image, though they too call themselves a center party.

3. We can have it unmistakably clear that _____ President is prepared to use force to restore order.

4. We believe we should begin with _____ small proposal that will provide job security leave to workers.

5. Each of these persons represents one member of _____ family unit.

6. _____ West German government today approved a bank loan to the Soviet Union.

7. In the Ukraine this week, people decided to do away with _____ Hammer and Sickle and fly their own flag.

8. It's _____ very difficult issue because real estate values are frozen.

9. We're going to continue to keep _____ close eye on what happens in Washington and California.

10. Share prices are heading south on _____ Tokyo Stock Exchange, hurt by a fall in the Yen and a weaker bond.

11. It is _____ new phenomenon for women with this life-threatening disease.

12. This is _____ Health Show.

Source: Data from Corpus of Contemporary American English.

Gap-Fill Activity

Answer Key

Fill in the blank with the *or* a.

1. **The** AAA survey which just come out today shows the falling price of gasoline.

2. The Free Democrats have **a** more radical, youthful image, though they too call themselves a center party.

3. We can have it unmistakably clear that **the** President is prepared to use force to restore order.

4. We believe we should begin with **a** small proposal that will provide job security leave to workers.

5. Each of these persons represents one member of **a** family unit.

6. **The** West German government today approved a bank loan to the Soviet Union.

7. In the Ukraine this week, people decided to do away with **the** Hammer and Sickle and fly their own flag.

8. It's **a** very difficult issue because real estate values are frozen.

9. We're going to continue to keep **a** close eye on what happens in Washington and California.

10. Share prices are heading south on **the** Tokyo Stock Exchange, hurt by a fall in the Yen and a weaker bond.

11. It is **a** new phenomenon for women with this life-threatening disease.

12. This is **The** Health Show.

<u>Source</u>: Corpus of Contemporary American English

Class Materials

SIGNAL WORDS

CONCORDANCE LINES FOR *so*

1. I wanna remind you that we do not have class on Thursday. This is to give you a chance to work on the midterm, so spend some time thinking about the midterm.

2. Women who work hard and earn less bring less home to their families. And so, the economic changes that have brought more and more women into the work force in the twentieth century have clashed with the inability of our society to deal with large numbers of women in the labor force.

3. Remember, surplus people are producing for surplus, and so the reduction for the need for women's labor occurs among young, unmarried women in the home who formed some of the early factory workers in the early stages of industrialization in New England.

4. Gradually the notion of women's work sort of gets erased. It's not paid labor in the home, and so it no longer is considered work.

5. Many of these young daughters began to continue to go through school till high school and then to college, and so we see a real change by the 1870s and 1880s in which women's colleges are drawing more young unmarried women into college educations.

6. During World War Two, with large numbers of men leaving home, there was an extraordinary labor shortage, and so government propaganda was produced to get as many women into the work force as possible.

7. I want it to be active knowledge so, in your essays, every time you are referring to an article that you read, put it in parentheses.

Source: MICASE

8. I'm gonna show you some pictures of it, but this area of Kenya is very arid, so you have to move in accordance with the seasons. When it's the dry season, you have to go to the few areas where there's a constant supply of water.

9. During the rainy season, you have more opportunities to go elsewhere and take advantage of different grazing areas. So, because of the environment, they have to have that mobility, and that mobility is increasingly infringed upon by these different factors.

10. All these communities which traditionally have been unregulated in their movements now are having to negotiate all these problems with ranches and government policies. So, because of all these increasing pressures on them from outside forces, it has led to an increase of conflict from within.

11. People say they work all the time, and so they don't have time to actually live life. They're too busy making a living.

12. If wealth is only the thing that you have, then it's hard for you to understand how you can still be wealthy after you've given all that stuff away. But in other societies, wealth is measured by many different things, so you can raise your status in society by having given away and redistributed your belongings to everybody.

13. They come from a different place and a different time, so sometimes virtually everybody that we'll be looking at historically, by the standards of today, would be considered a racist. But in the context of their time, some were and some were not.

14. You don't have to memorize this stuff; I'm offering this to you because it's a way of visualizing how it works, and so you can understand the process.

15. You have so many traits that may not give you valid information, so you just basically take all the traits and you weigh them all in various sorts of ways.

16. He was always seasick so you know he was always throwing up and he never could really sleep well.

17. He really didn't do much except sit at home and work whenever he could and think about the collections that he'd made. So, let's look at his ideas.

18. Once we have the general principles, they allow us to make specific predictions. So, once you decide that the reason that the sun rises in the east is because of the way the world is spinning, then you would predict the sun is gonna rise in the east again tomorrow.

19. There's a lot of bagels left, so feel free to come down at any time.

20. Now the structures are too big to write here, so what I'm going to do is I'm going to label them.

CONCORDANCE LINES FOR *then*

1. You not only have a vacation today, but you have a vacation on Thursday, and then we'll be showing a movie on Tuesday.

2. First came God, then came the king, and then came the heads of the families, okay? That's why when children went bad in the colonial period it was the father who was blamed, not the mother because he was responsible for everybody under him.

3. For younger daughters of New England farmers, it initially meant an ability to continue to contribute to the family economy. Some of them were able to earn dowries and then marry middle or upwardly mobile young farm men who were moving into the lower middle class.

4. Many of these young daughters began to go through school till high school and then to college, and so we see a real change by the 1870s and 1880s in which women's colleges are founded and drawing more and more, young unmarried affluent women into college educations.

5. But in the end, protective legislation was passed, first by the states individually and then eventually bolstered by the federal government.

6. I want you to understand and then be able to explain to us how those two things are constantly interacting.

7. And so, when governments go in, they wanna cordon off an area and say this is only for the exclusive use of tourists. Then, of course, that eats away again at traditional grazing areas that the Masai have always used. So that's yet another pressure.

Source: MICASE

8. They start as adolescent girls. Once they get married, then they are married women.

9. The example of a person in a chiefdom would be a chief who accepts contributions from everybody in a society and then redistributes it according to the needs of everyone in society.

10. Another example would be chiefdoms, where people'll harvest their own plots of land, but then at the end of the harvest they'll give a certain portion of that over to the chief.

11. The book then goes on to talk about cultural ecology and says how other people started theorizing consumption in terms of constraints given in the environment.

12. I just don't wanna do the wrong thing and then have somebody's lawyer call me in the morning saying, my client was recorded against his will.

13. I think that maybe there were lawsuits in the past and there were laws in the past, and then things changed, and now we have new laws.

14. That was the opposite in the sense of summarizing but then both of those ideas were out and a lot of more intelligent people thought that both worked.

15. Let me explain this to you, and again you don't have to copy this down, you can get it off the web when it's up, and then it'll give you a chance to review it because you can circle the stuff yourself.

16. Night is equal to the day in the spring and fall, and then in the winter, the sun goes south for the winter.

17. I interviewed fifty deans and faculty members and then four American student leaders to talk about what international students might be doing to influence the departments through the student groups.

18. First of all, you take in information; you learn about an issue; you notice it. Following that, you characterize, interpret, make some judgments about what's going on, and then, ideally, after that you respond based on this information.

19. Their needs are absolutely not considered. If you wanna stay here, then deal with our rules and if you don't want to, then that's fine, we've got many others that wanna take your place.

20. Because the plants that were in place to begin with were adapted to warmer environments and then slowly are changing through time, possibly the elevation hasn't changed enough during that period to influence the evolution of those plants as much.

CONCORDANCE LINES FOR *though*

1. The two disciplines do not appear on the surface to have very much in common. Historically, though, anthropologists and epidemiologists have worked together for a very long period of time.

2. Women are identified as being employed much less often than men. You can look at this as we live in a world where producers are conceptualizing women as dependent on men. Remember, though, you can also look at it as: men's characters may be disproportionately shown as being employed.

3. We're gonna verify this answer, and then we're gonna discuss a little bit about why it is so surprising. To verify the answer, though, I need some help.

4. How many of you saw that movie? Don't see it, the rest of you who haven't; it's pretty bad. Unfortunately, though, I have to say that I worked on that film.

5. The book made a nice guide to the movie. It is confusing, though, which I must say I find really kind of amazing when you realize the simplicity of the language.

6. The Department of Engineering has awarded four hundred PhDs since 1958, though only thirteen of those have gone to women.

7. The item I'm trying to sort might actually already be in the right spot. Let's say it isn't, though, and small is different from start.

Source: MICASE

8. It's a fairly old paper, so if you want a copy of the paper you can go read it. It's not required that you get this paper, though.

9. If I put in the discount factor, though, it's going to differ not only between this segment and this segment, but it's going to get heavier and heavier the older I get.

10. Now a lot of people who don't speak like my uncle have a few words that people who know him well can understand. For the most part, he doesn't speak. He can be an excellent mime, though.

11. Meanwhile, I'm eager to hear what she has to say tonight, because Joan Jacobs Brumberg tells a stunning and troubling story. What is even more important, though, is that she not only tells us a fascinating and disturbing story, but she has some important ideas about how we might do better, in providing what adolescent girls need to survive.

12. Diary keeping has almost always been a middle class activity for a variety of reasons that have to do with affluence and styles of nurture. What's interesting, though, about the history of diaries is that they appear regularly among different ethnic minorities at that moment in the family history when the family has achieved middle class status.

13. Any other questions about the movie? What'd you think of it? I sorta liked it. There's so much covered in it though; it's really worth talking about it.

14. Well, in the first large cosmopolitan site, as long as the student's putting out good research, doing well in classes, the people really don't care how and (who) the support comes from. In the second site, though, it's a very much of a concern.

15. In the cosmopolitan huge site, somebody told me that no one needs any special attention. In the second site though, I found they were more concerned about the individual student here.

16. And so what's in that dark streak? There have been several claims as to what could be in that dark streak. We, though, did our own analysis, and found that it was F-E-three-O-four.

17. There's a technological view though, but the other view is to try and think of the environment the way the animal sees it and to try and think about an animal's eye view of the environment.

18. If you visit Williamsburg, you'll be struck because all of the buildings are reconstructed in Georgian style, and they do vary between brick and wood. The vast majority of the structures in Williamsburg, though, are made out of wood.

19. Well, it's possible. I wouldn't say that he's wrong though, necessarily.

20. In her recent work, she is clearly interested in the ordinary vicissitudes of adolescence for girls in contemporary America. She retains, though, a concern about the potential for the deeper trouble that some girls end up in.

Gap-Fill Activity

Read the sentences. Fill in the blanks with so, then, *or* though.

1. You may be surprised to learn that New York was quite a bit smaller than Philadelphia in 1770. Its growth was driven by river and ocean trade. Its great period of expansion, _____, doesn't actually happen until later, after the Erie Canal goes in, in 1825, which connects it to the interior markets of the Great Lakes area and Midwest and upstate New York.

2. We only have fifteen minutes left. I have way more than fifteen minutes to say about anthropology and it's gorgeous out there. _____, let us stop now, enjoy your time, and I will see you in March.

3. The first thing I did is try to do a regression equation figuring that it might work. Turns out, _____, that it doesn't.

4. When he chose a profession, he became first a doctor, and _____ a scholar practicing medicine, and a scholar of Japanese.

5. You could score yourself if you want to, and _____ I'll collect it, and I'll present you with the aggregate data after spring break.

6. Okay, this is the schedule for today. I'm gonna lecture on women, and I'll finish up at around ten after eleven; _____ I will hand out the midterm, and I will discuss the midterm for a while to make sure that all of you understand.

Source: MICASE

7. The Purple Martin has really thrived on relatively minor attention from people. Their num-

   bers, _____, seem to have declined and not really recovered.

8. When they reached a certain smaller size of population, they just didn't reproduce,

   _____ their social behavior was disrupted.

9. Those peasants had access to the land, the seed, whatever tools they needed, _____

   they had access to the means of production, but they had to pay a certain amount of it back

   to somebody else.

10. With descendent A, they're growing faster over time. And with descendent B, the growth

    rate is slowed down, _____ they're growing slower in the same period of time.

11. New Orleans started off as an administrative center of the French colony of Louisiana. It was

    taken over by Spain, _____, in 1765 because of some complicated wars and political

    maneuvers happening in Europe.

12. So these public meetings took place, and the epidemiologists would say stuff, and the clini-

    cians would say stuff, and _____ the women in the community would say stuff too.

Answer Key

1. You may be surprised to learn that New York was quite a bit smaller than Philadelphia in 1770. Its growth was driven by river and ocean trade. Its great period of expansion, <u>though</u>, doesn't actually happen until later, after the Erie Canal goes in, in 1825, which connects it to the interior markets of the Great Lakes area and Midwest and upstate New York.

2. We only have fifteen minutes left. I have way more than fifteen minutes to say about anthropology and it's gorgeous out there, <u>so</u> let us stop now, enjoy your time, and I will see you in March.

3. The first thing I did is try to do a regression equation figuring that it might work. Turns out, <u>though</u>, that it doesn't.

4. When he chose a profession, he became first a doctor, and <u>then</u> a scholar practicing medicine, and a scholar of Japanese.

5. You could score yourself if you want to, and <u>then</u> I'll collect it, and I'll present you with the aggregate data after spring break.

6. Okay, this is the schedule for today. I'm gonna lecture on women, and I'll finish up at around ten after eleven; <u>then</u> I will hand out the midterm, and I will discuss the midterm for a while to make sure that all of you understand.

7. The Purple Martin has really thrived on relatively minor attention from people. Their numbers, <u>though</u>, seem to have declined and not really recovered.

8. When they reached a certain smaller size of population, they just didn't reproduce, <u>so</u> their social behavior was disrupted.

9. Those peasants had access to the land, the seed, whatever tools they needed, <u>so</u> they had access to the means of production, but they had to pay a certain amount of it back to somebody else.

10. With descendent A, they're growing faster over time. And with descendent B, the growth rate is slowed down, <u>so</u> they're growing slower in the same period of time.

11. New Orleans started off as an administrative center of the French colony of Louisiana. It was taken over by Spain, <u>though</u>, in 1765 because of some complicated wars and political maneuvers happening in Europe.

12. So these public meetings took place, and the epidemiologists would say stuff, and the clinicians would say stuff, and <u>then</u> the women in the community would say stuff too.

<u>Source</u>: MICASE

───────────────── **Whole Language Activities** ─────────────────

You will give a mini-presentation (30–60 seconds) describing your reasons for choosing to study English in the United States. Outline the ideas you will speak about in the space below. Use *so, then,* and *though* at least one time. Take brief notes to help you plan your speech. For the parts in which you plan to use *so, then,* and *though*, write complete sentences so that you can practice using these words in their most frequently occurring patterns.

You will give a mini-presentation (30–60 seconds) describing an important issue in your college major or interest. Outline the ideas you will speak about in the space below. Use *so, then,* and *though* at least one time. Take brief notes to help you plan your speech. For the parts in which you plan to use *so, then,* and *though*, write complete sentences so that you can practice using these words in their most frequently occurring patterns.

Class Materials

ACADEMIC VOCABULARY

- [ ] again
- [ ] always
- [ ] another
- [ ] Arkansas
- [ ] asked
- [ ] away
- [ ] boy
- [ ] call
- [ ] called
- [ ] car
- [ ] Central High
- [ ] class
- [ ] come
- [ ] day
- [ ] door
- [ ] down
- [ ] even
- [ ] eyes
- [ ] face
- [ ] Faubus
- [ ] feel
- [ ] felt
- [ ] few
- [ ] first

- [ ] friends
- [ ] front
- [ ] get
- [ ] girl
- [ ] go
- [ ] God
- [ ] going
- [ ] gonna
- [ ] good
- [ ] got
- [ ] governor
- [ ] grandma
- [ ] group
- [ ] guard
- [ ] hand
- [ ] head
- [ ] heard
- [ ] help
- [ ] home
- [ ] inside
- [ ] integration
- [ ] keep
- [ ] knew
- [ ] know

- [ ] let
- [ ] life
- [ ] Little Rock
- [ ] long
- [ ] looked
- [ ] mama
- [ ] man
- [ ] men
- [ ] moment
- [ ] morning
- [ ] mother
- [ ] Mrs
- [ ] myself
- [ ] new
- [ ] next
- [ ] nigger
- [ ] now
- [ ] once
- [ ] people
- [ ] really
- [ ] right
- [ ] rock
- [ ] room
- [ ] say

- [ ] school
- [ ] see
- [ ] segregationists
- [ ] soldiers
- [ ] something
- [ ] still
- [ ] stood
- [ ] students
- [ ] take
- [ ] talk
- [ ] tell
- [ ] things
- [ ] think
- [ ] though
- [ ] thought
- [ ] time
- [ ] told
- [ ] two
- [ ] voice
- [ ] walked
- [ ] want
- [ ] white
- [ ] words
- [ ] year

Source: Amazon.com Amazon Online Reader for *Warriors Don't Cry*

PowerPoint Slides for *major, area,* and *evident*

major

- *determiner+(adj)+major*
- negative nouns *(crisis, problem, catastrophe, change, fight, violence)*

area

- p. 8, 61, 62, 90, 95, 100, 107, 113, 138, 152, 248, 257, 300, 310
- *(in)+the/a+(adj)+area*
- negative *(isolated, dangerous, deprived)*
- size *(huge, large, small)*

evident

- p. 103, 175, 182, 190, 231, 274
- *(it)+was+evident*
- verbs—*be+evident, seem+ evident*
- prep—*evident+to+me, evident+from+noun/pronoun*

Class Materials

COMMA ERRORS

STUDENT INFORMED CONSENT

Example

I understand that _____ (instructor's name) will use my written work from _____ (course name/number) for in-class activities on errors in writing. My writing will remain anonymous (it will not be identified as mine), and I, my classmates, and other English language learners may benefit from the activity.

If you are willing to volunteer your writing for these activities, please sign below.

_____

Student's Signature   Date

_____

Instructor's Signature   Date

CONSCIOUSNESS-RAISING/NOTICING ACTIVITY

Concordance lines for comma errors

Melba suffered for all black people and people who sacrifice their lives for others are great warriors.

Melba was determined to fight for integration and determination is one of the characteristics of a warrior.

She had to give up almost all her hobbies for her new life and she was not supported by her circle.

Melba reacted with non-violence and this is an unbelievable thing.

Melba suffered not only for her benefit but also for the rights of all black people.

She did not like to let the segregationist do their thing but she knew not responding to them was the best thing.

Melba fought not only so she could attend a good school but also so all black people could attend a good school.

Some students refused to participate but Melba kept going forward.

Many people would have given up at that time but Melba was more perseverant than ever.

Melba knew she could die from the torture at Central High but she didn't give up as a warrior.

A warrior is not only someone going to fight but someone who fights till the end.

Melba went through a wild life at Central High like having her peers chasing her.

Seeing that there were people opposing their presence in Central High some students refused to participate.

The fact that some students seeing that there were people opposing their presence in Central High...

Once inside Central High Melba accepted to not fight back.

When she attended Central High Mebla felt responsible for the inconveniences.

Even though her life was changing she had one general goal to reach.

Second, as a young person she really did not like to stand there.

Even though what she endured was too much for a little girl the result was worth it.

When Melba was with the other Little Rock Nine their conversation became different.

Melba faced serious dangerous segregationist actions such as being kicked.

Later she was surprised by how everybody refused her invitation on her birthday.

For example Melba had decided to bring her sandwich to eat in a safe place.

Thus Melba was a real warrior.

Once more the fact that some students…

Source: Learner Corpus

Traditional Grammar Activity

Sentence Types

1. <u>Simple Sentence</u>: 1 independent clause

   The student discussed her paper with the instructor.

   The student and her instructor discussed her paper and planned another conference.

2. <u>Compound Sentence</u>: 2 independent clauses (joined with a coordinator or transition word)

   The student writes every night, and his high grades reflect his hard work.

   Jane got up at 8 a.m.; unfortunately, she still missed the bus.

3. <u>Complex Sentence</u>: 2 independent clauses (joined with a subordinator)

   Although George works 25 hours a week, he does not earn enough to purchase a car.

   George does not earn enough to purchase a car although he works 25 hours a week.

4. <u>Compound-Complex Sentences</u> 2 independent clauses and a subordinate clause (joined with a coordinator or transition word and a subordinator)

   After Maria reviewed her notes, she thought she was ready for the test, and she was right.

   Maria reviewed her notes, and she thought she was ready for the test until she studied with her friend.

———————————— **Traditional Grammar Activity** ————————————

Conjunction Chart

Coordinators		Transition Words and Phrases		Subordinators	
Coordinators are used to connect two independent clauses.		Transition words and phrases are also used to connect two independent clauses. They show more specifically than coordinators how the ideas of the two clauses are related.		Subordinators are used to connect an independent clause and a subordinate clause.	
for	*or*	*also*	*however*	*although*	*because*
and	*yet*	*besides*	*nevertheless*	*even though*	*since*
nor	*so*	*further*	*in contrast*	*after*	*if*
but		*in addition*	*even so*	*before*	*unless*
		moreover	*otherwise*		*even if*
		therefore	*next*	*when*	*like*
		thus	*then*	*while*	*as*
		as a result	*finally*	*until*	

Source: Modified from http://oregonstate.edu/dept/eli/march1997.html

Authentic Language Activity

Proofreading

Melba's life changed drastically as a result of attending Central High School. She could no longer do things like a normal teenager, her friends changed and some of her family traditions were ruined.

For one thing before Melba attended Central High School she would go to the wrestling matches on Saturday nights. Now she could not attend because it was too dangerous. When she was attending Central High Melba's New Year's resolutions included "to stay alive" when most teenagers just want to get a boyfriend or girl-friend. Second Melba's old friends were scared of being around her; they did not even attend her birthday party. However Melba made new friends with the other Little Rock Nine. They became such good friends, they thought of each other as family. The last way Melba's life changed was some of her family traditions were ruined. For instance she could not do her regular Christmas shopping because two boys threat-ened her at the store. Later her special Easter dress was ruined by a segregationist.

Even though Melba's life changed drastically as a result of attending Central High School she was glad to be a part of integration.

References

Azar, B. S. (2009). Personal correspondence, 14 December.

———. (2002). *Understanding and using English grammar,* 3rd ed. New York: Pearson Longman.

Bamford, J., & Day, R. (2004). *Extensive reading activities for teaching language.* Cambridge, UK: Cambridge University Press.

Barlow, M. (2007). MonoConc Pro 2.2 [Computer software]. Houston, TX: Athelstan. www.athel.com/mono.html

Bennett, G. (2006, Spring). Much ado about literature. *Washington Association for the Education of Speakers of Other Languages, (31)*2, 9–11. www.waesol.org/newsletters_files/2006_2_Spring.pdf

Biber, D. (2005). *Corpus linguistics and language teaching: The next lexus.* Paper presented at the 39th annual TESOL convention, San Antonio, TX.

Biber, D., Conrad, S., & Reppen, R. (1998). *Corpus linguistics: Investigating language structure and use.* Cambridge, UK: Cambridge University Press.

Biber, D., Johansson, S., Leech, G., Conrad, S., & Finegan, E. (1999). *Longman grammar of spoken and written English.* New York: Longman.

Brown, H. D. (2001). *Teaching by principles: An interactive approach to language pedagogy.* New York: Longman.

Byrd, P. (2007). *Collocations and recurrent phrases in the academic word list.* Paper presented at the 41st annual TESOL convention, Seattle, WA.

Byrd, P., & Reid, J. (1998). *Grammar in the composition classroom: Essays on teaching ESL for college-bound students.* Boston: Heinle & Heinle.

Carter, R., & McCarthy, M. (1995). Grammar and the spoken language. *Applied Linguistics, 16*(2), 141–158.

———. (2006). *Cambridge grammar of English.* Cambridge, UK: Cambridge University Press.

Conrad, S. (2000). Will corpus linguistics revolutionize grammar teaching in the 21st century? *TESOL Quarterly, 34*(3), 548–559.

Cortes, V. (2007). *With or without corpora.* Paper presented at the 41st annual TESOL convention, Seattle, WA.

Coxhead, A. (2000). A new academic word list. *TESOL Quarterly, 34*(2), 213–238.

———. (2007). *The Academic Word List: How to use this list.* Victoria, New Zealand: School of Linguistics and Applied Language Studies, Victoria University of Wellington. www.victoria.ac.nz/lals/staff/averil-coxhead/awl/howto.html

Davies, M. (2008). Corpus of Contemporary American English, www.americancorpus.org.

Day, R., & Bamford, J. (1998). *Extensive reading in the second language classroom.* Cambridge, UK: Cambridge University Press.

Ferris, D. (2008). Students must learn to correct all their writing errors. In J. Reid (Ed.), *Writing myths: Applying second language research to classroom teaching* (pp. 90–114). Ann Arbor: University of Michigan Press.

Fredricks, L., & Sobko, V. (2008). Culturally relevant extensive reading in Tajikistan. *Central Eurasian Studies Review, 7*(1), 34–39. Retrieved October 26, 2008, from www.cesr-cess.org/pdf/CESR_07_1.pdf

Granger, S. (1998). *Learner English on computer*. London: Longman.

———. (2003). The International Corpus of Learner English: A new resource for foreign learning and teaching and second language acquisition research. *TESOL Quarterly, 37*(3), 538–546.

Green, J., & Oxford, R. (1995). A closer look at learning strategies, L2 proficiency, and gender. *TESOL Quarterly, 25*, 375–406.

Hüning, M. (2008). TextSTAT (Simple Text Analysis Tool) 2.8 [Computer software]. Berlin: Freie Universitat. http://neon.niederlandistik.fu-berlin.de/textstat

Hunston, S. (2002). *Corpora in applied linguistics*. Cambridge, UK: Cambridge University Press.

Hunston, S., & Francis, G. (2000). *Pattern grammar: A corpus-driven approach to the lexical grammar of English*. Amsterdam: John Benjamins.

Iwahori, Y. (2008). Developing reading fluency: A study of extensive reading in EFL. *Reading in a Foreign Language, 20*(1). Retrieved April 16, 2008, from http://nflrc.hawaii.edu/rfl/April2008/iwahori/iwahori.html

Jacobs, G. M., & Gallo, P. (2002). Reading alone together: Enhancing extensive reading via student-student cooperation in second-language instruction. *Reading Online 5*(6). Retrieved September 7, 2007, from www.readingonline.org/articles/art_index.asp?HREF=jacobs/index.html

Johns, T. (1997). Contexts: The background, development and trailing of a concordance-based CALL program. In A. Wichmann, S. Fligelstone, T. McEnery, and G. Knowles (Eds.), *Teaching and language corpora* (pp. 100–115). London: Longman.

Jones, L. (2001). *Let's talk*. Cambridge, UK: Cambridge University Press.

Kennedy, G. (1991). *Between* and *through*: The company they keep and the functions they serve. In K. Aijmer and B. Altenberg (Eds.), *English Corpus Linguistics: Studies in Honour of Jan Svartvik* (pp. 95–110). London: Longman.

Kozyrev, J. R. (2002). *Talk it over! Listening, speaking, and pronunciation 3*. Boston, MA: Heinle Cengage Learning.

Lea, D. (Ed.). (2002). *Oxford collocations dictionary for students of English*. Oxford, UK: Oxford University Press.

MacWhinney, B. (1992*). The CHILDES database*. Dublin, OH: Discovery Systems.

McCarthy, M. (2004). *Touchstone: From corpus to course book*. Cambridge, UK: Cambridge University Press.

McCarthy, M., McCarten, J., & Sandiford, H. (2005). *Touchstone 1*. Cambridge, UK: Cambridge University Press.

Merdinger, P., & Barton, L. (2009). *NorthStar listening and speaking 1* (2nd ed.). New York: Pearson Longman.

Mindt, D. (2000). *An empirical grammar of the English verb system*. Berlin: Cornelsen.

Nation, P. (1997). The language learning benefits of extensive reading. *The Language Teacher Online 21*(5).

O'Keeffe, A., McCarthy, M., & Carter, R. (2007). *From corpus to classroom: Language use and language teaching*. Cambridge, UK: Cambridge University Press.

Pattillo Beals, M. (1995). *Warriors don't cry: A searing memoir of the battle to integrate Little Rock's Central High*. New York: Washington Square Press.

Scott, M. (2004). WordSmith Tools 4.0 [Computer software]. www.lexically.net/wordsmith/version4/index.htm

Sinclair, J. (1991). *Corpus, concordance, collocation*. Oxford, UK: Oxford University Press.

———. (2003). *Reading concordances*. London: Pearson Education.

———. (2004). *How to use corpora in language teaching*. Amsterdam: John Benjamins.

Thornbury, S. (2004). *Natural grammar*. Oxford, UK: Oxford University Press.

White, M. (2007). A good story in 50 words? *The Language Teacher, 31*(5), 19–20.

Widdowson, H. (1990). *Aspects of language teaching*. Oxford: Oxford University Press.

Zwier, L. J. (2002). *Building academic vocabulary*. Ann Arbor: University of Michigan Press.

Zwier, L. J., & Bennett, G. (2006). *Teaching a lexis-based academic writing course: A guide to building academic vocabulary*. Ann Arbor: University of Michigan Press.

Index